B E Y O N D
MENTORING

Comprehensive Induction Programs

How to attract, support, and retain new teachers

Jon Saphier
Susan Freedman
Barbara Aschheim

*TEACHERS*²¹   2345 WASHINGTON STREET, NEWTON, MA 02462   617/552-5393

ISBN 0-9715587-0-1

Copyright © 2001 by *TEACHERS* 21

To order copies of this book or to request reprint permission, please contact *TEACHERS* 21, 2345 Washington Street, Newton, MA 02462 (617) 552-5393   teachers21pubs@aol.com

TABLE OF CONTENTS

- The national teacher shortage

- A push for high standards

- Expanded demands on administrators' time

- The challenges that schools face

- A mutual benefit

- The flaws of informal approaches: A scenario

- The comprehensive model

- A comprehensive approach: A scenario

- The philosophical underpinnings

- What is meant by a "comprehensive" approach?

- A guide for school districts

TABLE OF CONTENTS

TABLE OF CONTENTS

TABLE OF CONTENTS

FORWARD

Modification of an African proverb:
It takes a whole district to raise a teacher.

Beginning teachers do not start out proficient. They are novices, no matter how mature they are personally or how rigorous their academic background. Nor should we expect anything else. We do have a right to expect that they emerge from their preparation programs with deep content knowledge of their subjects – although there is reason to doubt in many cases that this is happening.

But, there is an array of proficiencies we would be foolish to assume and presumptuous to expect. Beginning teachers do not know how to set expectations, shape interpersonal climate, and teach routines during the opening days of school. How could they, never having had responsibility for doing so? In most cases, they have not been in classrooms at all during the first days or weeks of school, despite going through student teaching or intern experiences.

Furthermore, they do not know how to manage all the complexities of movement and flow in classrooms that are designed for active learning.

- They do not know how to differentiate instruction for students with different learning styles.

- They do not know how to respond to disruptive students or parent complaints.

- They do not know what to do on back-to-school night or in parent conferences.

- They do not know how to motivate low performing students who doubt their own abilities and believe they are incapable of meeting high standards.

None of the above is criticism of beginning teachers or the institutions that prepare them. Novices are not supposed to know all the complexities of their craft at the beginning. It is, however, our responsibility to them and to the children they serve to provide them in their early years with the conditions for learning and reflection that are congruent with complex practice. We need to provide them with a comprehensive array of supports that ensure that they will be successful and that the children in their classrooms have an optimal opportunity to learn.

A comprehensive induction program involves more than just mentors. In fact, mentors alone, though a critical part of good induction, cannot hope by themselves to provide the range of input, feedback, and support beginning teachers need. Well-designed induction programs include specific roles for principals, superintendents, central office personnel, the teachers' union, parents, school board, and particularly the other staff members in the school or department where the beginning teacher works.

Nothing is more important to the learning of students than what their teachers know, believe, and can do. The pivotal importance of teachers to student achievement has been documented (Darling-Hammond/National Commission on Teaching and America's Future, 1996; 1997). What has been absent in the career paths of American teachers is the recognition that their work is intellectually complex, difficult, and demanding on a par with other developed professions – law, architecture, medicine. We do not provide the many forms of support for beginning teachers that they need to grow into proficient professionals. Only the most durable survive the first few years, especially in our cities; and the rate of growth toward proficiency is far slower than it could be, at great cost to our children (See Chapter One).

In these pages, we provide a map for planning a comprehensive induction program for beginning teachers in their first three years of practice. This program includes seven components:

1. Criteria based selection and matching of mentors

2. Services for mentors: training, supervision, support

3. Services for beginning teachers: courses, support groups, resources, feedback, coaching

4. School board and community understanding and support that is visible through budgets and policies

5. Services for and from principals: enlisting the whole staff to support new teachers

6. A district-wide planning process that designs and then provides for the management and assessment of the induction program

7. On-going and well-designed program assessment

This book also describes in detail the roles that superintendents, principals, teachers, school board members, central office administrators, and others must play in a well-designed and comprehensive induction program. It is a practical guide for implementing the induction programs our beginning teachers and our children deserve.

Such a program is within the grasp of any American district now; in addition, resources are being provided in many states explicitly to fund local units for improving the ways that they support their new teachers (Darling-Hammond, 2001). The vision that follows does not call for large quantities of new resources, though induction may require re-examining their distribution if there is no outside aid. While some districts will need to start one component at a time, we hope all districts will embrace and benefit from the comprehensive planning process that we describe in this book.

ACKNOWLEDGEMENTS

The development of an effective, comprehensive model for the induction of beginning teachers needs to be based in real practice in large, small, urban and rural school districts. We are very appreciative of the many school administrators who have welcomed us into their districts to help facilitate the development of district induction plans and the implementation of their induction programs. The suggestions, creative thinking, and cautions of these educators have greatly enhanced our thinking about this model.

We also have appreciated the thoughtful critiques of the individuals who have generously given of their time to review this book:

Members of the *Teachers*[21] Board of Directors:

Lynn Stuart, Principal of the Cambridgeport School in Cambridge (MA) and a member of the National Commission on Teaching and America's Future

Matt King, Superintendent of the Wellesley (MA) Public Schools and a *Teachers*[21] consultant

Lyndy Johnson, Assistant Dean of Graduate Education, Simmons College and co-founder of the Beginning Teacher Center of *Teachers*[21] and Simmons College

Other *Teachers*[21] consultants:

Peg Mongiello, Principal, Blake Middle School in Medfield (MA)

Rob Traver, Director of the Beginning Teacher Center of *Teachers*[21] and Simmons College

Jennifer Antonucci, former Assistant Principal, North Middlesex Regional High School (MA)

Our colleagues in other educational organizations:

Kathleen Kelley, President of the Massachusetts Federation of Teachers

Donald Rebello, President, Massachusetts Secondary School Administrators Association and Principal of Somerset (MA) High School

Our appreciation also goes to **Kathleen Butler** for bringing to our attention the Harrison and Bramson framework on communication between people who are engaged in problem-solving.

Technical support that was critical to the success of this book came from our office manager, **Dan Price**, who provided on-going logistical support and technological expertise, and our graphic designer, **Beth Heppenstall**, whose good judgment, skillful eye, and patience contributed to the final product.

CHAPTER ONE

Why Comprehensive Induction?

Across America – in large and small cities, counties, and in suburban and rural areas – a call has gone out for new teachers. As a country, we are experiencing one of those employment cycles that catches everyone's attention.

- Cherished veteran teachers are retiring.

- The baby-boomers are having children in record numbers, resulting in large "bulges" on school district population charts.

- Some of the new teachers hired to teach these children are leaving the profession after only one or two years of teaching, making the teacher shortage worse.

The National Teacher Shortage

In 1996, the nation was estimated to have 2.7 million teachers, over 50% of whom would be retiring by 2003. It is widely agreed that between 1995 and 2003, American schools will be hiring approximately

2.4 million teachers and that by 2007 there will be 3.3 million teachers in American schools (Darling-Hammond, 1996). Approximately 20-30% of the teachers who were in schools in 1995 – and who may have spent a career in these schools – retired by the year 2000. Another 20-30% of these veterans will be retiring between 2000 and 2005.

As veteran teachers retire, school districts are struggling to find well-prepared newcomers who are ready to take on the challenges of teaching in today's demanding classrooms. In earlier generations, it was an easy decision for many college graduates to become a teacher. The abundant career options that are available today for women and men did not exist. The days in which most women had the limited choice of working as a "teacher, nurse, or secretary" are long behind us. The expectation that young people would stay in town and work in the factory or the schools has similarly disappeared.

The new teachers who seek to replace these veterans are finding that there are big shoes to be filled. As a result, school districts are faced with the challenge of retaining the talented newcomers that they bring into their buildings. The expectations are high, the hours are long, the paper work is unending, and the isolation of the classroom can be demoralizing. Linda Darling-Hammond, in *What Matters Most: Teaching and America's Future*, reports that 20-30% of new teachers who do not have support are leaving the profession in the first 5 years. Even more alarming, over 50% of the teachers in urban schools who do not get support are leaving in the first or second year. Out of every 600 students entering four-year teaching programs, only 180 complete them, only 72 become teachers and only about 40 are still teaching several years later. The problem is not only recruiting teachers; it's retaining them – and that problem points to some very real shortages (Gregorian, 2001).

A Push for High Standards

At the same time, there is a strong movement in this country for higher standards for student achievement and greater accountability for that achievement on the part of classroom teachers. Today's teacher works with a broader spectrum of learners in his or her classroom than has been the case for many decades. "Inclusion" and "mainstreaming" programs – coupled with the elimination of "gifted and talented" classes – means that the job of the teacher is to provide meaningful learning experiences for a wide continuum of learners.

Pick up a newspaper or news magazine in most states in this country and you will read about the increased testing that is taking place – for students and for teachers. Teachers in all 50 states are sharply aware that each year their students will be tested in statewide assessment programs that are linked to their state's mandated or recommended curriculum. The results of this testing in some states are used to determine funding for local schools and to measure the effectiveness of individual teachers. New teachers must be able to show results and show results quickly.

Expanded Demands on Administrators' Time

School principals, department heads, superintendents, and other administrators who have traditionally been responsible for supporting the new teachers they hire are unable to devote the time and attention to their newcomers that they could when they were hiring only one or two a year. Now, with 5-15 new teachers a year in many schools, administrators have much less time to help novice teachers become familiar with the expectations and programs of the school. These administrators' days are filled with long lists of responsibilities that include supervising and evaluating new and veteran staff, providing leadership for effective instruction, marshaling resources for the schools, and managing parent involvement in the life of the schools.

The Challenges that Schools Face

The stakes have been raised for districts as they seek to retain the talented new teachers they hire. The push to raise standards, greater accountability for students and teachers, and the broader range of learning needs that children bring to the classroom are challenges that make teaching more complex and difficult than at any other time in our nation's history.

The teacher is unarguably the single most important factor in schools that helps students reach high levels of performance (Sanders and Reeves, 1998; Gross, 1999). With unprecedented numbers of new teachers in our schools, how are we going to ensure that they have the support, information, and skills they need to be effective? Will superintendents, other administrators, school committees, and the larger school community commit themselves to the planning and allocation of resources that will provide new and veteran teachers with sufficient time, training, and supervision to nurture and support the next generation of teachers?

A Mutual Benefit

Several decades of research on the experiences of new teachers indicates that 95% of those novices who are provided with support are likely to remain in the profession (Bartell and Ownby, 1994). The idealism and energy that they bring to their career can be nurtured and sustained, even when the going gets tough. The support of a caring and experienced mentor, professional development programs that acknowledge and understand that they still have lots to learn, and opportunities to meet with other new teachers to problem-solve and troubleshoot can make the difference between leaving in frustration and having a rewarding and successful first year of teaching.

Numerous studies and surveys indicate that new teachers who are provided with support are more likely to involve students in more complex learning experiences, make better decisions about curriculum, manage classroom discipline more effectively, and willingly engage in reflective practice about their teaching. The mentors who work with these newcomers also report significant benefits from the experience. Mentors repeatedly note that their own teaching is improved – if not transformed – by both the process of thinking and talking about their own practice and by the ideas and techniques that are learned from the new teacher (Scherer, 1999). In successful programs, new and veteran teachers find that their mentoring partnership is a mutually beneficial relationship.

A final benefit speaks directly to teaching as a profession. The mark of a profession is how it supports and holds high standards for its practitioners. Think of other professions you come across daily – doctors, lawyers, accountants, architects, nurses, and more. The professions they belong to take responsibility for supporting their professional growth and for helping to induct new members through internships, apprenticeships, residencies, and other training programs. Teaching will have more of a claim on professional status when teachers, administrators, and school boards together take responsibility for providing new teachers with the support they need.

The Flaws of Informal Approaches

In 1999, the Oldtowne Public Schools found that they needed to hire 27 new teachers in one year. This turnover was unprecedented, as until now the district had only seen one or two retirements each year. In 1999, however, twenty teachers reached retirement age, two received maternity leaves, and five additional teachers were needed because of growth in the student population.

Superintendent Jayne Thompson asked all principals to develop their own plans for supporting the new teachers whom they had hired for their schools. At the high school, department heads were asked to give extra support to the new teachers in their departments. At the middle school, which was organized into clusters, teachers were asked to include new teachers in all cluster planning activities and a few veteran teachers offered to serve as informal mentors to newcomers who shared their teaching areas. Three of the six elementary schools had three or four new teachers each. The principals in these schools asked specific teachers — who taught the same grades as the new teachers — if they would be mentors to the new teachers.

At the end of the school year, the superintendent surveyed the new teachers and the mentors to determine the effectiveness of the program. New teachers reported that they received the most assistance with personal or moral support, strategies for dealing with specific students, and ideas for curriculum and instruction. The department heads and mentors reported that the activities that they most frequently engaged in with the new teachers included providing personal and professional support, strategizing about the needs of specific students, and techniques for motivating students. Some mentors also noted that beginning teachers gave them new ideas for curriculum and helped them with their computers.

Allowing for some variations, the experiences that the new teachers had in Oldtowne were not different from experiences that teachers have had for decades in informal mentoring relationships. In the beginning of the school year, administrators pair new teachers with veterans. Perhaps the pairs are given guidelines on how often they should meet, what these meetings should be about, and what the goals are for the experience. Perhaps not. Little is said about the expectations that the principal has for the relationship or the areas of teaching that the pair will explore together. The mentor is not given guidance in how to proactively discuss the strategies of successful teaching and the protégé is not encouraged to ask for help. As a result, the mentor provides strong emotional and personal support for the new teacher and the new teacher, hopefully, is comfortable asking lots of questions that open up the veteran teacher to sharing her extensive body of teaching knowledge.

What's missing in this picture?

The *ad hoc*, informal nature of traditional mentoring scenarios rely heavily on the initiative, instincts, and good will of the veteran teacher and the protégé. The need to support, nurture, and retain new teachers for today's challenging classrooms requires that we become more intentional with the approaches we take to induction.

Beginning teachers who are not paired with a specific mentor report that early in the school year they begin to feel that they are a burden on their colleagues. How many times can they expect their veteran colleagues to be willing to listen to their problems? How often can they intrude on their veteran colleagues' time to ask for advice or ideas? School administrators cannot assume that by putting in place a support program – by pairing mentors and beginning teachers –

their vision for collegial and professional support will result. Administrators need to understand the many unique opportunities they have to protect and support the beginning teacher and the mentoring pair. Through scheduling, student placement, the locations of classrooms, and the assignment of duties and extracurricular activities, principals and department heads are able to impact the nature of the mentoring relationship. The ways that administrators use these structures in schools also signal to their staff the importance that they place on supporting every new teacher in their building.

Mentors need to know what the district expects of them as transmitters of the culture and wisdom of teaching. Experience shows that most mentors need training and support in the critical role that they play in helping new teachers use their energy, enthusiasm, idealism, and intelligence in ways that promote student learning (See Chapter Four).

Beginning teachers also need to know that the district values their efforts to become quality teachers. Indeed, they are not being left on their own to discover the mysteries of teaching. There is a system in place – a plan – that has been designed to support them – as newcomers who have more to learn and as professionals who have knowledge and ideas that can enrich the teaching of both the new and veteran teachers around them.

CHAPTER TWO

A Comprehensive Model for the Induction of Beginning Teachers in Their First Three Years of Teaching

The Comprehensive Model

Teachers[21] has developed a **comprehensive model for the induction of beginning teachers** that is gaining adherents and demonstrating results. It suggests that support for new teachers needs to be a priority of school administrators and needs to happen in a systematic way. It brings together in a coherent plan the many different ways that schools can support their new staff members – and the veterans who are helping to support these newcomers. It is based on the assumption that everyone in the school community needs to understand their responsibility for reaching out to new teachers and providing them with the encouragement, resources, beliefs, and attitudes that will contribute to their success in the classroom.

A Comprehensive Approach

It was clear to Superintendent Clare Ramirez and Assistant Superintendent Deborah Wong in 1997 that the Glendale Public Schools were going to be hiring record numbers of new teachers in the next five years. It was also clear that they would be competing with their neighboring communities for the candidates they wanted for their classrooms. To respond to this need and to ensure that the candidates they hired were successful in their schools, they formed a steering committee to explore the directions they wanted to take and to develop an induction plan for the district. The superintendent, others from the central office, school principals, the president of the teachers association, and veteran teachers came together to participate in a workshop on the research on mentoring programs. This training included an orientation to the needs and stages of beginning teachers and the skills and expectations of mentors.

With this knowledge as a foundation, the group participated in a planning process that identified the goals of the district induction program, the qualifications of mentors, criteria for matching beginning teachers with veterans, the expectations of the mentor-protégé pair, and the training and other forms of support that would be made available to the new teachers and their mentors. With this plan in place, the Glendale schools are providing new teachers and their veteran colleagues with a coherent program of support that is attracting strong candidates, strengthening the performance of newcomers, revitalizing veteran staff, and enhancing student achievement.

The Philosophical Underpinnings

Mentoring programs are not new. For decades, principals have asked respected veteran teachers to be mentors to newcomers. Once they were paired, the mentor and the protégé were basically left on their own to carve out a relationship that was satisfying and useful. Rarely were they formally linked to other resources in the school and rarely did other folks in the school feel that they had a responsibility to the new teacher since he or she "already had a mentor."

What is Meant by a "Comprehensive" Approach?

This comprehensive induction model presents an enhanced vision for induction:

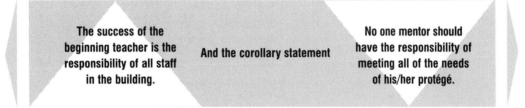

The success of the beginning teacher is the responsibility of all staff in the building.

And the corollary statement

No one mentor should have the responsibility of meeting all of the needs of his/her protégé.

All staff in the building need to understand that they play an essential role in the success of the beginning teacher. With this understanding in place, we might see...

- Teachers opening their classrooms for observations and their file drawers for curriculum materials that will be helpful to the beginning teacher.

- Teachers conferring with the beginning teacher on strategies for meeting the needs of specific students.

- Teachers sharing their approaches to classroom management and discipline.

- **Structures, time, and leadership for these things to happen.**

A comprehensive program is developed with involvement from a broad base of school administrators, teachers, and the teachers union. No longer does the induction program depend on the initial enthusiasm of a few dedicated administrators or teachers for its survival. It becomes institutionalized as an integral part of the professional development program of the district.

TEACHERS[21]
Model for the Induction of Beginning Teachers

Criteria Based Selection and Matching of Mentors

Mentor Services

- Training
- Supervision & Support

Beginning Teacher Services

- Beginning Teacher Courses
- Beginning Teacher Support Groups

District Wide Planning Process

- Central Office
- Administrators
- Teachers Union
- New & Veteran Teachers

Administrator Services

- Strategies for Whole Faculty Involvement
- Skills for the Supervision & Development of Beginning Teachers
- Support for Mentors

School Board & Community Development

Education, Policy and Financial Support

On-going Program Assessment

Foundations for the Model:
- Professional Knowledge Base on Teaching
- Constant Strengthening of Professional Community

Figure 1.

How is a comprehensive induction program organized and implemented?

The heart of a comprehensive model of induction is a plan, as can be seen in Figure 1. Representatives from all of the constituencies in the school engage in a **planning process** that delineates criteria, qualifications, and standards for the induction program (See sample plan in Appendix A).

A coherent program of staff development and networking is designed for mentors, beginning teachers, and school and district administrators. This training and networking is based on the best information that we have – through research and practice – on the **Knowledge Base on Teaching**, on **developing building-wide support for beginning teachers**, and on **successful mentoring**.

- **Mentors** participate in workshops that strengthen their skills in providing positive and negative feedback to colleagues. They also update and refine their knowledge base on the district curriculum and on the latest research on teaching and learning.

- **Beginning teachers** attend workshops on classroom management, curriculum, and teaching strategies that bridge the gaps that so often emerge between their teacher preparation programs and the realities of their first three years of teaching.

- The mentor-protégé relationship is strengthened through **collegial activities** that could include sharing ideas on curriculum and instruction or formal and informal observations in each others' and other colleagues' classrooms. These collegial interactions provide professional support to both the new and the veteran teachers and can help to strengthen the culture of the whole school as a learning community.

- **Superintendents, principals, union leaders,** and **other school administrators** participate in institutes that focus on the unique opportunities they have to build a school culture in which all teachers believe they have something of value to offer the beginning teacher. They expand their understanding of strategies for facilitating colleague-to-colleague observing, conferencing, and planning. They also receive training on techniques for ensuring that their excellent new staff receive developmentally appropriate supervision and evaluation.

- **School Board** members receive information that briefs them on the significance and design of comprehensive induction. They are asked to form policies and budgets to support the program.

- Superintendents, central office administrators, union leaders, and principals use their **existing communication vehicles**, such as newsletters, cable-tv, web pages, letters home, and articles in the local newspaper, to broadcast the benefits of their induction program. These vehicles help teachers, administrators, parents, students, and others in the community know the goals and objectives of the program and understand it as a valuable asset of the school district.

- **Formal and informal on-going evaluation** ensures that the program is meeting the needs of beginning teachers and mentors and that it is producing the intended results.

A Guide for School Districts

This booklet will guide the reader through the components of a comprehensive program of support for new teachers. It will share experiences and strategies in order to help the reader anticipate the process and be prepared to adapt this model to his/her own district circumstances.

CHAPTER THREE

The Components of a Comprehensive Induction Program

Our comprehensive approach to the support of new teachers has seven components. In laying out these components, we will present the planning function last – while in reality it would occur first.

Not only should planning happen first, it should be understood as the crucial activity that ensures that comprehensive induction programs work. Without it, the pieces don't click, support for those involved is erratic or missing, and no "flight controller" feeds essential information to the pilots to keep the plane on course.

However, to be ready to plan, teachers and administrators need to be clear on the goals they want to achieve through their plan. What is the vision for new teachers? For mentors? For administrators? What might a mentor pairing program look like? What kinds of training are needed? What kinds of structures need to be put in place in schools?

For this reason, we will start with the pieces of a program and then move to the planning that holds these pieces together. This exposition may, in reality, more closely reflect the situation in your community. Perhaps you already have a good start. You may already have mentors; you may already have some support activities in place for beginning teachers; you may already have pto presidents recognizing the accomplishment of completing the first week of teaching by delivering roses to new teachers. Once you have reflected on the strengths that exist in your schools, you will be ready to undertake the important process of planning.

Component 1:
Criteria Based Selection and Matching of Mentors

The Application and Selection Process – Make it Something Special

We recommend that teachers apply and go through a selection process to become mentors. This process involves circulating criteria and expectations for this important responsibility. It also inserts, when there are enough candidates, an element of rigor and competitiveness into the process, thus elevating its status.

We further recommend that the district use inclusive processes for recruiting mentors that include inviting all teachers to attend an orientation training that describes the roles and expectations for mentors. Mentoring programs are most successful when all teachers have the opportunity to volunteer to participate. The research is also clear that mentors need training on their role as a mentor and on supporting beginning teachers with effective approaches to classroom practice. While not all teachers who apply and who participate in training may be selected in a given year to become mentors, the process helps them understand the expectations of mentors and the ways that they can support the mentoring pairs in their schools. Because the training we recommend incorporates large components on observation and feedback, this effort to train mentors can also positively impact school-wide collegial behaviors (See page 56 for a definition of collegial behaviors).

A rigorous selection process allows teachers and administrators to become clear about the role of the mentor and administrators to communicate these clear expectations in advance. In addition, having an application process signals that not everyone can be a mentor; it is an important position for which people must show competence and commitment. At the same time, of course, superintendents, principals, and other administrators should feel free to urge individuals whom they believe have the appropriate knowledge, skills, and attitudes to apply for these positions with the understanding that candidates will still go through the selection process.

Districts may want to consider the following sample criteria and expectations:

Criteria

- Proven track record as a successful classroom teacher with over three years experience

- A communication style that adapts to individual differences

- Behaviors that show commitment to constant learning about the craft, collegiality, and experimentation in one's teaching

- Demonstrated perseverance and confidence building with resistant students and slow learners

- Strong belief that effective effort is the key determinant of student success

- A long-term commitment to the mentoring role and to the protégé

- Commitment to the completion of a program of study that builds skill in observing, analyzing, diagnosing, and being articulate about skillful teaching

Comment: Since mentors will observe beginning teachers at work and help them analyze problems, it is very useful if mentors have a common language and conceptual framework for talking about teaching. We have included the idea of a common language in the "criteria" section because of our belief that the study of teaching itself should be part of the background of a teacher who is qualified to be a mentor.

Expectations

- Will complete in the first year a 36-hour course in Mentor Skill Training

- Will engage in subsequent years in an additional 36 hours of advanced mentor training

- Will be available for a total of approximately 2 to 3 hours per week to work with mentee

Comment: We suggest that the 2 to 3 hours per week that is recommended for mentor-mentee meetings be applied flexibly. It is not necessary to schedule rigidly the three hours; what is necessary is that the mentor connect with the beginning teacher often, ask how things are, and be willing to debrief and/or bolster confidence when needed. In any given week, this may add up to three hours of time.

- Will observe mentee or otherwise be present in mentee's classroom at least once weekly

- Will make appointments for one-on-one conferences with mentees – approximately weekly – to check in and explicitly deal with mentee's problems or issues. These conferences are scheduled as opposed to the lunch meetings, conversations in the hall, or other brief (though possibly very important) conversations that will take place during the day. The purpose of the conference is usually to meet the mentee's agenda.

- Will take turns leading monthly seminars on topics of concern or interest to the mentees as a group (e.g., parent conferences, Back-to-School Night, teaching math). Seminars will be scheduled for "late days" or on Study Group Day.

- Will demonstrate lessons or management techniques on request

- Will link beginning teachers with other resource people in the school and district

- Will follow the beginning teachers through their second and third years of teaching with appropriate support services

Mentors should be relieved of certain duties (e.g., bus duty, recess supervision, study halls, detention) to provide the time the job of mentoring demands. The mentor's planning, correcting, and preparation load is not reduced when one becomes a mentor. Therefore, some compensatory time needs to be found to enable mentors to do their new job well. Stipends are appropriate for mentors and should represent a meaningful amount of compensation. We recommend approximately 5% of a teacher's base pay or other recognition as described in Appendix B. Because mentors should represent the highest level of professional excellence in the district and because the work of supporting the newest members of the professional community is extremely important, we believe that it is appropriate to provide significant recognition and appreciation for this extra work of these valued colleagues.

Maintaining Logs

The application process may also require the mentor and the protégé to maintain time logs of their meetings – and observations – to demonstrate that they have met the standard that was set by the district. Many districts provide a form on which the dates can be recorded. Some districts also ask for a one-word description of the focus of the meeting or observation (curriculum; classroom management; parent communication). This information provides data for the district on the needs of beginning teachers while not breaching the confidentiality of the mentoring relationship.

Mentoring Log

Date	Time	Topic	Comments?
8/28	9:15	Start up issues	
8/29	2:30	Attendance formats	
9/7	7:45; 3:15	Classroom management	
9/9	8:05	Rules and routines	
10/4	2:30	Back to school night	
10/6	7:50	Back to school night	

Matching Mentors and Protégés Carefully

The traditional wisdom on matching has stood the test of repeated research and practical experience:

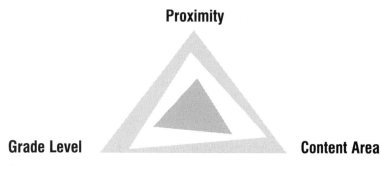

Proximity

Grade Level　　　　**Content Area**

When matches are based on this triad, **grade level**, **content area**, and **proximity**, they provide the best support for new teachers in terms of child development, classroom management, and curricular and instructional expertise. Proximity provides the ability to be immediately responsive to the new teacher as well as available for informal discussions before and after school, during hall duty, and at other "down" times during the school day. Matches are also more likely to be successful when the pair shares professional, social, and personal interests.

In many districts, matching is done by the principals who have hired the new teachers. Because the principals are assumed to have a good knowledge of the teachers in the building and of the new hires, they often want the responsibility for making these matches. In other districts, matching is done by a school-based committee which includes the principal. Occasionally, a central office administrator, such as the mentor coordinator or an assistant superintendent, has this responsibility.

The "Blind Date"

For too many teachers, the mentor pairing process results in a "blind date." The teachers do not know each other and neither partner has input into the pairing.

Recommendations

- Circumvent the blind date:
  - The interview team. Principals invite potential mentors for a particular position (third grade teacher; science teacher) to participate in the interview process as members of an

interview team. Through this interaction, some pairings are able to be made based on natural "affinity."

– The "sock hop" approach. New teachers and prospective mentors spend a day together in workshops and social activities in August that enable them to become at least slightly acquainted. New and veteran teachers are encouraged to "find comfortable partners" in their grade level or content area during the day with whom they may apply to be matched. This "pairing off" allows teachers to find colleagues with whom they have some initial "chemistry."

• Provide for "no fault bail out." What if, with the best of intentions on all sides, the match does not work? Sometimes two good teachers find that their styles or their personalities do not match and that the pairing is mutually unsatisfactory. The "no fault bail out" process enables the pair to talk with a neutral person – usually not the school principal who supervises them – to ask that they be reassigned to other teachers. In many districts, the curriculum coordinator, a guidance counselor, or the mentor coordinator serves as this "neutral person" who may provide some mediation with the pair to determine if the match can be salvaged. If not, a new pairing is made "with no prejudice" toward the pair.

Confidentiality

A sensitive and important issue for both beginning teachers and mentors is the issue of confidentiality. Mentors should not be put in the role of evaluator or be expected to report to principals how things are going with the novice teacher. Beginning teachers need to be confident they can reveal their fears, disappointments, and vulnerabilities to a trusted mentor who will use this trust as a springboard to help, not injure. Yet, there must be boundaries to confidentiality when the interest of children is at stake. Therefore, we recommend the statement below as a policy document defining confidentiality between mentors and beginning teachers:

Confidentiality Statement

In general, mentors will not discuss their protégé's teaching performance with anyone, including school and district administrators, except under the following conditions:

1. Mentor teachers will be able to discuss, with the protégé's knowledge and permission, any aspect of their protégé's performance with other members of the mentoring team – i.e., the principal or teachers or administrators who may be designated as resources for the new teacher.

2. Mentors, with the protégé's knowledge and permission, may discuss the protégé's teaching performance with resource professionals whose job it is to help teachers.

   (For example, if the novice needs help in designing hands on science lessons, the district science coordinator may be consulted for help and advice.)

3. Mentors, with the protégé's knowledge, may discuss the protégé's teaching performance with appropriate administrators if, in the mentor's professional judgment, the academic growth and development, social well-being, or physical safety of the students is at risk.

Teachers[21]

Superintendents, principals and other administrators in districts should receive training on the principles that underlie confidentiality so that they have the same understandings as do new and veteran teachers about how the confidentiality policy works. Supervisors and evaluators are reminded that the presence of a mentor in no way changes their responsibility to provide support and guidance to new teachers on a regular basis. They must understand that the mentor should not be expected to be a source of information on the performance of the beginning teacher. Their evaluations of new teachers must be based on their own first-hand knowledge of the new teachers' performance.

Component 2:
Services for Mentors

The core of support for mentors is good training coupled with periodic opportunities to problem-solve and share cases with other mentors. In addition, it is essential that mentors have the time they need to do the job and that they receive recognition and appreciation for their work.

Training: Seven Modules

Figure 2 shows the topics we recommend for mentor training. While the sequence is not critical, it is important. Mentors must have completed some training before they take on the responsibility of working with a beginning teacher. We recommend that in each of the first two years of mentoring, veteran teachers take a 36-hour course that provides the knowledge base and skills needed by an effective mentor.

The **first module** in this training provides important baseline information about the roles and responsibilities of the mentor and research data on the impact that good mentoring relationships have on the success of beginning teachers.

The **second module** explores the communication styles mentors will find useful throughout their lives, but especially when problem-solving with mentees. Individuals of our species have very different thinking and communication styles that show up when identifying and solving problems. For example:

- Some people like to generate masses of alternatives before beginning to weigh what should be done.

- Others want to linger over the definition of a problem and a vision of the outcomes that could result from the solution before spending any time brainstorming ideas.

- Some people think through their ideas by talking out loud without intending to signify that they have taken a position; they may sound like they're taking a position, but they're only thinking aloud.

- Other people do their thinking and sorting inside their head, and only speak when they have a position which they want to float.

These are four tiny examples of a larger constellation of variables that characterize thinking and talking behavior during problem-solving. Two people of opposite styles working together can drive one another crazy – or get into unnecessary conflicts if they don't understand their partner's communication style. Knowing your own and your mentee's style makes the relationship much more productive: you understand and are more tolerant of behaviors that would otherwise irritate you, and you and your mentee can also adjust to one another. There are a number of frameworks upon which to base this kind of training. We recommend Harrison and Bramson's model (Harrison and Bramson, 1982) since it focuses on communication between people working on problems in the work setting.

Mentor Skill Training
72 Hours over 2 Years of Basic & Advanced Training

Module 1– Role of Mentor

All about beginning teachers (needs, stages...)

All about mentor-protégé relationship (e.g., confidentiality)

Rapport and trust

Overview of mentoring skills

Course expectations, ground rules

Introduce belief system

Role of Mentors in Comprehensive Induction Programs

9 hours

Module 2 – Communication Style

Thinking style, problem-solving style

Harrison and Bramson (similar framework)

Matching communication style to mentee

6 hours

Module 3 – Differential Conferencing

Develop the relationship through support, help, problem-solving

Differential leadership styles
(Sweeney, Hersey & Blanchard, Edmonds, Glickman)

Case studies of matching along the collaborative/directive continuum

Active listening

Using data to define the problem

Active listening + probing for specificity in problem-solving conferences

Role-plays of problem-solving

Feedback exercise from cognitive coaching

Modeling and role-playing 3 kinds of conferences: non-directive, collaborative, directive

Focus on directive conferencing and delivering negative information

18 hours (includes basic and advanced topics)

Module 4 – Developing Mentee's Planning Skills

Alignment of objectives, learning experiences, assessment

Alignment with curriculum frameworks

Backwards planning: *Do it. Coaching and helping others do it.*

12 hours

Module 5 – Diagnosing and Solving Planning & Management Problems

Space, time, routine momentum, attention, expectations and consequences, motivation

9 hours (includes basic and advanced topics)

Module 6 – Advocacy

Helping the mentee deal with:

1. principal 2. difficult people
3. conflicts with other staff 4. role in school

3 hours (advanced)

Module 7 – Plan

Action plan by month

6 hours (advanced)

Module 8 – Guardian of Values

Responsibility and accountability

Personal efficacy

Constant learning

Mission, repertoire and matching

Collegiality and interdependence

6 hours (advanced)

Module 9 – Working with Administration & Mentor Leaders

3 hours (advanced)

Figure 2.

You will note that a significant section of the mentor training is devoted to the **third module** of "differential conferencing." Once a mentor has achieved some capacity in adjusting for the communication style of his mentee, it is then easier to examine the degree of directness vs. indirectness that should be used with a beginning teacher. "Differential Conferencing" refers to the need for mentors to vary their approach to feedback and coaching along a continuum that has supportive and collaborative at one end and directive on the other, depending on the professional maturity of the beginning teacher. (Professional maturity means a teacher's level of experience and wisdom in decision-making within a particular field and has nothing to do with personal or emotional maturity.)

Many mentors enter their roles believing that their only legitimate relationship with mentees is as coach. Their understanding is that to be a coach means to be supportive, to be led by the mentee's agenda, and precludes giving negative feedback or suggestions. The "Cognitive Coaching" model of Costa and Garmston (1994) is one we heartily endorse and include in our training. It teaches how to use data and questions to stimulate the thinking of the observee. It should not be misunderstood, however, to mean that a mentor should never be directive and that the observee must always come to his/her own conclusions about what the problem is and what needs changing or improvement.

The progression from novice to expert in any knowledge-based field is described by Benner (2000) and Dreyfus & Dreyfus (1986). Novices do not have large repertoires of behaviors for handling the multiplicity of decisions that are called for in many different areas of performance. Nor do they have the lenses for reading the environment and perceiving patterns of behavior that suggest clear interpretations and courses of action to experts (Shulman, 1986;

Berliner, 1987). Thus novices tend to function from "rule governed behavior" (See Figure 3). Over time, as their competency increases, their capacity to make situational decisions increases as does their repertoire of ways to respond in different situations.

Our goal in feedback and coaching is to develop novices' capacity to analyze and make decisions. Thus, it is never out of place to use data about what happened in the class to bring the mentee's attention to events they may have missed; it is never out of place to ask good questions to stimulate their thinking and decision making capacity. It is also not out of place in certain situations to tell them what to do and how to do it, especially if they are floundering. This is the perspective of "differential conferencing."

Model of Change & The Development of Expertise

(Edmonds adapted from Dreyfus)

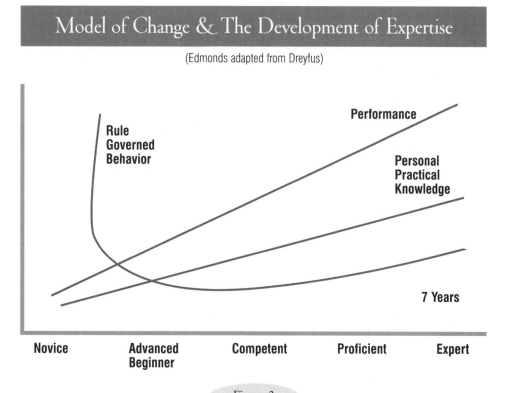

Figure 3.

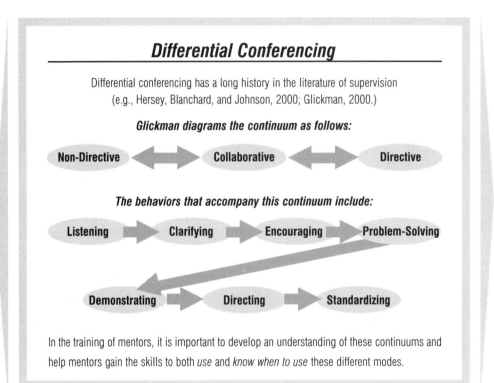

The **fourth module** of mentor training bears on the beginning teacher's planning skills. Despite college courses and student teaching, we find many beginning teachers have gaps in the logic and precision they bring to the alignment of learning experiences and objectives – i.e., between the activities they choose or design for students and the knowledge and skills they want students to attain.

Successful teaching is built on a clear image of exactly what one wants students to know and be able to do at the conclusion of the lesson or unit. This image must be communicated to students, ideally with exemplars of what good work will look like. And, finally, one must be able to show that the activities the students are asked to do can logically be expected to lead to the intended learnings!

Surprising as this may seem to some readers, many activities that teachers have students do – even experienced teachers – are engaging, active, fun... and not really connected with the objectives – or at least not closely enough connected. They are the teacher's favorites, or the kids' favorites, or the ones in the manual. Mentors need to develop their own skills so that they are able to coach new teachers on effective planning and thinking skills. (Excellent examples of teaching to learning outcomes are provided by Wiggins and McTighe, 1998.)

It will be no surprise that the **fifth module** helps mentors diagnose and solve classroom management problems with beginning teachers. Being a good classroom manager oneself is no guarantee one can help another become proficient. Great players do not always make good coaches. This module gives mentors the skills to analyze and be articulate about the nature of classroom management problems. It gives them the vocabulary and conceptual framework to help beginning teachers see the nature of a problem and generate new responses.

The **sixth module** prepares mentors to advocate for their mentees and enable their mentees to advocate for themselves when conflicts arise with other adults in the school community. Mentors are prepared to identify the situations that may arise and to draw on the skills of honest, open communication and mediation where necessary.

Mentors are provided, in the **seventh module**, with suggestions and strategies for developing a plan for their work with a beginning teacher over the course of the year. Knowing their school calendar and schedule, goals, and priorities, mentors develop a monthly plan that tracks the needs of beginning teachers and that ensures that interactions with the beginning teacher include a balance among all of the essential issues such as classroom management, lesson planning and instruction, collegial relationships, and professionalism.

The **eighth module** has a "values-driven" dimension, even though its fruits show up concretely in very specific and practical circumstances. This module is about influencing the belief systems of beginning teachers. It is a crucial topic because, ultimately, all our decisions and actions spring from our beliefs... about ourselves, about children, about learning, and about what it means to be a professional. We recommend that mentors discuss the following beliefs with their protégés:

Beliefs for Influencing the Next Generation of Teachers

Responsibility and Accountability

If the children aren't learning, I can't blame them or their life circumstances. It is my responsibility to keep examining my curriculum and my teaching to reach these children.

Personal Efficacy

I can be successful as a teacher and help these children experience success. I can do it.

Constant Learning

Teaching is intellectually complex, difficult, and demanding work. It is expected that I ask for help and consult colleagues frequently, both as a beginner and as a veteran. No one knows everything there is to know about teaching, or ever will. Constant learning is the name of the game.

Mission, Repertoire, and Matching

There is not one right or best way to do something in teaching. Skillful teaching means continually enlarging one's repertoire and getting ever more accurate at picking from one's repertoire to match the student, the situation, or the curriculum.

Collegiality and Interdependence

Effective professional practice requires true collegial behavior among teachers. It is expected of me and I expect it of my colleagues in return. I know that we need each other to produce effective work for children. I also know that we as a grade/department/school faculty have cumulative school-wide effects.

Mentors have opportunities to influence these beliefs in several ways that have nothing to do with services for the beginning teacher. The opportunities show up in the flow of everyday life and their normal interactions with their protégés. The first way to influence is through modeling. Mentors are encouraged to be aware of how they speak about their own teaching, their own students, their colleagues, and their own process of learning from their practice. If we were to listen in on them talking about these topics, we would conclude they have the beliefs listed above.

A second opportunity to influence beliefs is in faculty room conversations. What does the mentor do if a teacher at the lunch table describes a student to the beginning teacher in one of the following ways:

> *"I sympathize with you. I had him last year, and he simply hasn't got the brainware. Put your time and energy into the good students!"*

> *"Well, you know that family. What can we expect?"*

In this module for mentors, we role-play interventions for these situations. Mentors cannot let such a moment pass without pushing back on the implicit belief about the student's capacity that is being passed on to the beginning teacher. And yet, one wants to preserve good relations with one's peers without being excessively confrontive. How does a mentor speak out in a responsible way?

In addition, during this module we examine other arenas – faculty meetings, grade level and department meetings, and parent conferences. In all of these settings, the beginning teacher's beliefs may be challenged or influenced. The role of mentor training is to coach and support mentors to effectively challenge the beliefs of others.

The **ninth module** focuses on the mentor's skills and knowledge in regard to building relationships with school administrators and the induction program coordinator. Mentors expand their understanding of how the induction program works, the roles of school and building administrators, and the opportunities that they have to strengthen and enhance their local program.

Rewarding and Appreciating Mentors

To stipend or not to stipend is a question asked by many districts. It is our belief that mentors, who represent the most respected teachers in the schools, should be recognized for the important work they do in supporting new teachers. Elsewhere we have recommended a 5% salary increment. However, this recognition can take many forms and – sometimes – is available in a menu format from which the mentor makes selections (See Appendix B).

The factors that go into the decision range from the precedents in the district on how teachers are rewarded for work they do outside of the classroom to alternative approaches to recognizing teachers that may or may not involve financial remuneration.

The work of the mentor is not easily contained in neat packages of time. For this reason, mentoring is not like coaching a team, advising a school club, or serving on a committee. While a minimum amount of time for conferencing and observations is usually specified, most mentors find that they spend substantially more time with their beginning teachers than the minimum that is required. For this reason, it is our experience that stipends should not be related to the time that is anticipated or to "hourly rates" that may be specified for other extracurricular work in contractual agreements. Rather, the stipend should be based on a percentage of the mentor's salary.

For some districts, it may be feasible to provide a variety of options to the mentor. Mentors may choose to have some compensatory time and a reduced stipend. They may desire to have a reduced course load and serve as a mentor to more than one beginning teacher. The permutations can become very creative once a range of ideas are presented for consideration.

Regardless of the form of reward that is provided, mentors should also be visibly and frequently acknowledged:

- Presentations to the school committee on the program can include reports by a few mentors and their protégés.

- Newsletters to parents should introduce the mentors and explain their role in supporting the professional practice of new teachers.

- The parents' organization, the teachers union, or others could partner with the superintendent and others in the administration in providing appreciation events such as a dinner or coffee at the start or the end of the school year.

- At faculty meetings, mentors can report on their involvement in the program and encourage other teachers to network with their beginning teachers.

Component 3
Services for Beginning Teachers

"As one of my questions during my interview, I asked the principal if there was a mentoring program for new teachers. She told me that she felt very strongly about the importance of pairing each new teacher with a highly respected veteran. She also told me about workshops that were designed specially for new teachers. It became clear to me that all new teachers were expected to participate in these programs for new teachers. I was delighted, because it said to me that I was not expected already to know everything I needed to know to be a good teacher. This was a district I wanted to work in."

Beginning Teacher

The Hiring Process

The induction of beginning teachers starts with the interview. As with hiring for any position, tone, expectations, and attitudes are communicated in the first interview.

In January 2000, *Education Week* reported that 28 states required that school districts provide an induction program for new teachers. It is not surprising, therefore, that for the last five years, it has been fairly routine for teacher candidates to inquire in the interview about the existence of a support program for beginning teachers. Most teachers know about these services from their teacher preparation programs or from professional magazines and journals. The district that can point to the quality of its induction program for new teachers is at a substantial advantage in the currently competitive employment environment.

In some districts, one condition of hiring is that the new teacher will accept the support of a mentor and will participate in staff development programs for new teachers. In other districts, new teachers are "cordially invited" to take advantage of these programs that have been put in place to support their successful introduction into the profession and the school district.

Expectations for Beginning Teachers

During the hiring process, candidates for teaching positions should be told that they will be paired with a mentor and expected to participate in programs designed to support beginning teachers which will include weekly observation and feedback from the mentor, coursework designed for new teachers, and periodic problem-solving sessions. This message should convey the district's strong commitment to ensuring that new teachers are successful and that they have the professional support they deserve and need as novices in this district.

The Orientation of New Teachers

How are new teachers welcomed...

Into your school district?

Into your school?

Into the fourth grade cluster or the social studies department?

Does your school have a building-wide program for new teachers that complements the district-wide welcome at the beginning of the year?

As school districts have found themselves hiring new teachers in large numbers, they have refined their beginning-of-the-year orientation programs. For many new teachers, orientation takes several forms that are described below.

Information "Dumps"

Too often, new teachers start the year at district-wide meetings where they are subjected to a massive "info-dump" from the administration. This meeting usually starts or ends with the distribution of massive three ring binders and assorted colorful handout sheets. Teachers report that too often the information has minimal relevance for them at that time – or that they can not absorb the information because of the pressure they are feeling about the start of the school year. They also note that the carefully compiled materials very often are placed on a desk or the floor and then become the foundation for a tall stack of materials that may – or may not – be read on the weekend preceding school – or at any time during the school year.

Recommendations

- Take a cue from "just in time" training. "Just in time" information is meted out to teachers on a schedule that tracks their need for the information.

- Develop a school schedule and calendar that highlights the important dates for which teachers need to be prepared. The accompanying forms and details are distributed closer to the time that they will be needed (See Appendix C for a sample school calendar designed for beginning teachers).

- Provide introductions to district policies and procedures at the building level, as it is in the school that these policies and procedures are usually implemented.

Introductions to the Local Community

The percentage of new teachers who live in the community usually numbers less than 50%. These new hires may be strangers to the city or town.

Recommendations

- Organize a bus or van tour that points out the neighborhoods, the popular hangouts, local museums, parks, and other features that can be resources for the classroom. It is equally important to point out banks, drugstores, markets, and other sites that can be time-savers and conveniences for busy new teachers.

- Provide a map of the school and give tours of the facilities. New teachers appreciate being informed about the resources in the building that they may want to use during the year.

Introductions to the School Community

With many schools having experienced a turnover of 50% or more in the last five years, administrators are instituting new approaches for helping new and veteran teachers get to know each other. These approaches are also helpful to students and parents.

Recommendations

- Have a staff social before school starts. Provide each beginning teacher with a designated host – not the mentor – who will introduce them to other staff. Highlight the beginning teachers during the event.

- Have all faculty members wear nametags for the whole first two weeks of school to help beginning and veteran teachers get to know who's who, especially in big schools.

- Put up bulletin boards with pictures of the new staff – or all staff.

- Using scanners and computers that are available in most schools, print "face books" that are similar to the booklets that colleges develop each year for their students. Both new and veteran teachers appreciate having this handy reference booklet at their desks.

Courses for Beginning Teachers

In the box on the next page is the outline of a course for beginning teachers which we recommend. Before commenting on the content and sequence of the course, we will offer a few points on the nature and approach of such a course.

In any profession, there are different kinds of knowledge one needs to be a fully functioning practitioner. Appendix F, The Knowledge Base on Teaching, outlines six such areas for teaching: content knowledge; content specific pedagogy; differences in learners; parent and community relations; professional community; and generic pedagogy.

Beginning Teacher Institute

Day 1. Creating an Effective Environment for Learning

- Developing a welcoming climate
- Organizing the classroom for high performance learning
- Beliefs for the next generation of teachers
- Holding high expectations for all students

Day 2. The Basics of the First Day, Week, and Month

- Preparing for the first days of school
- Identifying and implementing initial planning and teaching tasks
- Planning classroom procedures and routines
- Effectively using the principles of time management

Day 3. Positive Classroom Management

- Tools for successful classroom management
- Diagnosing classroom discipline problems
- Teaching and learning strategies that motivate students

Day 4. Building Partnerships with Parents

- Communicating with parents
- Helping parents support their children's learning
- Meaningful homework assignments

Day 5. Lesson Planning

- Key elements in lesson planning
- Developing lessons that meet the needs and styles of diverse learners
- Lessons for higher order learning

Day 6. Linking Curriculum and Assessment

- Exploring the Curriculum Frameworks
- Aligning teaching, learning, and assessment
- Using multiple approaches to student assessment

Beginning teachers can benefit from learning in all these areas, but there are clear priorities in the first year. In the area of generic pedagogy, the following areas are first order needs: classroom management; room set up; establishing expectations and climate; and detailed plans for the first day and first week.

By mid-October, Back-to-School Nights are held and the first parent conferences are looming. Specific sessions with experienced teachers on how to handle these events are in order.

"What do parents really want to know on back to school night?"

"How do experienced teachers organize their presentations for back to school night?"

"Parents want to know something about who you are. More importantly, they want to be reassured that you know who their children are and care about them."

"Detailed outlines of the curriculum may not meet parents' needs. They want to know that you are organized and know what you are doing."

Simulated sessions, including role-plays, are invaluable in preparing for parent conferences. Veteran teachers also can show beginning teachers samples of student work that they have available for parents to examine during the Back-to-School Nights and parent conferences.

Another emphasis in the first year is to ensure that beginning teachers learn "mastery planning." An increasing number of beginning (as well as experienced) teachers are very knowledgeable in their academic discipline and may know many diverse instructional strategies. However, they do not necessarily choose or create learning experiences for children that are precisely aligned with their objectives.

Professional development for beginning teachers must ensure that they are proficient at aligning objectives, learning experiences, and assessment precisely. This approach to lesson planning is also called "Backward Design" (Wiggins and McTighe, 1998). It can help beginning teachers have a clear image of what they want students to know and be able to do at the conclusion of individual lessons (as well as at the end of a series of lessons and units). From this vision, they choose or design experiences which can logically be expected to lead students to the desired learning. This skill cannot, regrettably, be taken for granted.

Beginning Teacher Network

The **Beginning Teacher Network** is a safe place to bring problems such as a professional conflict with a department chair, a difficult interaction with a parent, or an insecurity about an aspect of one's teaching. In the Beginning Teacher Network, a small group of 4-6 teachers meets for an hour, 10 times throughout the year, in a confidential session that is designed to address their needs and to raise issues related to their professional responsibilities. These sessions may be led by an experienced practitioner from outside the school district or by a trusted veteran teacher or administrator from within the system.

Topics that are explored by the Beginning Teacher Network could include:

- Negotiating professional relationships with colleagues
- Balancing the goals of the written curriculum with the "hidden" curriculum that is advocated by administrators
- Involving parents in meaningful roles in the classroom
- Personal time and resource management

Services for Second and Third Year New Teachers

New teachers who are in their second and third years profit from staff development that expands and deepens their knowledge base and skills. With a year of experience behind them, these teachers are ready to delve into issues related to curriculum, instruction, and assessment.

Professional development that is particularly appropriate for second and third year teachers includes:

- In-depth exploration of literacy and numeracy at the elementary level through workshops and study groups

- Coaching on interdisciplinary approaches to curriculum

- Training on expanding teachers' repertoire of content-specific pedagogical approaches

- Guided examination of data and its use in strengthening student learning

- Course work on Teaching in a Standards-Based Classroom; Differentiated Instruction; and Student Performance Assessment

- Training on team building and working collegially with peers

Component 4
School Board and Community

To sustain a comprehensive induction program through good and bad economic times, and over the tenures of new and different school board members, care needs to be taken to make induction a part of the culture and the budget of the district. This is not easy.

We made the case at the beginning of this book that nothing is more important to student learning and achievement than the quality of teaching. Therefore, when budgets get tight, the cuts must not come in programs that influence this quality. Elected school boards must be educated with convincing data about the significance of teaching quality. The explicit connection must be made between a good induction program and its impact on good teaching by new teachers. Statistics on strengthening teacher retention, which we cited in Chapter One, are important, but just the beginning.

Presentations

We are advocating, first, that a presentation – perhaps a series of presentations – be made to the school board to convince members that quality teaching and the role of good induction in creating this teaching should be at the top of their priorities. These presentations need to be repeated, perhaps at regularly scheduled dinner meetings, every time new board members are elected. They also need to be given in community living rooms, at neighborhood coffees, and at rotary clubs and other forums to provide a level of support for the school board when it needs to make difficult budget decisions in lean times.

Policy

Second, when the job of educating the school board has reached a satisfactory point, we recommend the superintendent or a school board member propose that the board include in its policy manual a statement that explains that comprehensive induction is a commitment of the district. Such a policy might read as follows:

> The superintendent will annually review the effective functioning of the district's Comprehensive Induction Program and report the current status to the School Board.
>
> The School Board will ensure adequate funding for the on-going training and support structures of the induction program.

Budget

Third and finally, we recommend that a line item labeled "Induction Programs" be included in the annual budget and become part of the boilerplate used for budget planning each year.

It must be clear that we are looking at influencing organizational structures, such as policy and budget, in order to institutionalize the district's commitment to comprehensive induction. Little could be more important for influencing the experience of children in our schools.

Component 5
Enlisting the Whole Staff: A Key Role for the Principal

A friend once said we wouldn't need mentors if the whole staff adopted the beginning teacher as its own. The idea was that everyone could be mentors in a workplace properly structured for professional practice.

While we still think there is a need for a trained mentor who creates a special relationship with an individual beginning teacher, there is great merit to being self-conscious and deliberate about getting the whole staff to "adopt" the beginning teacher. Let us pose this question for building leaders, especially principals.

What would you do if you wanted every member of your staff to believe...

1) Every teacher has a stake in the beginning teacher's success.

2) Every teacher has something of value to offer the beginning teacher.

Let's get more specific. It's April. What can you do between now and the orientation at the beginning of the next school year to accomplish the two goals above?

Class Placement and Scheduling

By April, we usually know how many openings there will be at each grade level and in each department. We urge school leaders to participate in class placement directly so that new teachers are assigned students and classes that are appropriate to their beginner status.

This means, bluntly, that you make sure that **new teachers do not get:**

- Stripped down classrooms

- Large classes

- Difficult students

- Many preparations for each day

- A heavy load of extracurricular assignments

It also means that **new teachers do get schedules that allow for:**

- Common planning time with their mentors for conferencing and other meetings

- Opportunities to observe and be observed by their mentors

Ask teachers who are moving students on to the new teacher's classroom to attach personal notes – one or two sentences – that tell something useful about each of their student's learning style.

> *"Works well in small groups, especially if you give him a leadership role. Otherwise, he might try to lead them anyway by cracking jokes."*

> *"Needs encouragement to bolster self-esteem."*

This is the kind of information that does not show up in cumulative records that are passed forward with students.

Start with the Interview

It is not an exaggeration to say that supporting, nurturing, retaining, and acculturating the new teacher starts at the interview. There has been a tidal shift in what candidates are expecting to learn in the interview on how the school and the district are prepared to help them to be successful in this new job.

The interview gives the administrator several opportunities to:

- Share a vision for educating children

- Describe the culture of the school – the values, beliefs, and attitudes that are shared by school staff

- Describe the staff development opportunities that are provided by the school and the district

- Outline the ways that this school supports teachers who are new to the school or new to the profession

It also provides a vehicle for launching the new teacher's involvement in the district induction program. It is most appropriate to use the interview to:

- Set expectations for new staff in regard to their participation in the activities and services of the induction program, such as workshops, meetings, and the mentor pairing program

- Provide veteran teachers with an opportunity to meet with new teachers – as part of an interview panel or post-interview socializing, for example – to help take some of the guesswork out of the matching process

- Demonstrate the administrator's commitment to supporting new teachers to be successful by giving examples of how this support is given

Provide and Protect Mentor-Beginning Teacher Time Together

Beginning teachers should be excused from committee assignments to the maximum degree possible so they can concentrate on the all-important first year task of learning their curriculum and how to teach. Similarly, mentors should have other committee assignments minimized so they can focus on their mentee. The three hours a week they will devote to their beginning teacher will be carved out of their hides unless their administrators see to it that the time is carved out of their schedules. This is especially important if no stipend or release time is provided to mentors. If a mentor stays with a mentee through the second and third year, the time commitment may diminish for this veteran teacher – who may then be able to take on another first year teacher.

Superintendents and principals should also keep a protective eye out for scheduled events that will conflict with either beginning teacher or mentor meetings – and be clear that induction program sessions take precedence when conflicts occur.

Enlist the Staff

Use faculty meetings in the spring and fall to get the staff thinking about the beginning teachers. Here are some ideas:

"I Remember"

Start a faculty meeting with "I Remember," a reflective activity you model with a partner first.

You and a partner stand in front of the staff. You say a sentence about something you remember from your first year of teaching.

> *"I remember how when I started I wanted to right all the wrongs that teachers had done to me as a student."*

Then your partner takes a turn.

> *"I remember how my first year I had no life...preparing lessons and correcting papers every night and weekends."*

Then you take another turn.

> *"I remember how Jason Bullworth locked the supply closet while I was inside and I couldn't figure out whether to yell bloody murder or wait a minute until another teacher came in for stuff."*

You each take three turns, starting your one or two sentence remarks with "I remember..." The whole modeling takes about 1 1/2 minutes.

Ask the faculty to pair up with partners and simultaneously repeat what you modeled, speaking from their own recollections. Give them about four minutes.

This activity warms everyone up for you to give them a brief talk on how important it can be to have people watching out for you and helping you along that first year. You can ask them for suggestions on how together you can create conditions at this school so that your beginning teachers can have that experience.

"I Wish I Knew Then"

Ask each faculty member to write down seven things they wish they'd known when they started teaching their first year. Have everyone say one item out loud as you go around the room. Collect the lists and have them typed up, eliminating duplicate items. Pass them out at the next faculty meeting to kick off the continuing discussion of how everyone will take a part in supporting the new teachers.

Alternate version: Ask the staff to identify the things we veterans may take for granted that new teachers will need to know.

Cards in a Basket

Ask each faculty member to write on a card the best teaching tip they ever got. Ask them to sign the card. Collect the cards in a basket. Leave the basket in the teachers' lounge. Rule: anyone can look at the cards but you can't take a card away. If you read a card and it isn't clear to you what the person meant, ask them. Request they flesh out what they said on the card so that the beginning teacher who reads it next fall will know fully what they meant. The purpose of the activity is to make the cards maximally useful to the incoming beginning teachers. But there's a tacit agenda too. From the beginning, guess who wants to look over all those "best teaching tips?" Your veteran staff! This activity accomplishes two things. It gets your veteran staff learning from one another, talking to one another, and, because of the feedback and clarification process, makes the tips more understandable to a third party reader – such as the beginning teachers. This basket serves as a resource in future years, too, and can be supplemented annually.

Other Ideas

- Ask faculty members to write on a card something in their teaching that they would be willing to share, demonstrate, teach to, or have a beginning teacher observe. Post these cards in the teacher's lounge in the fall on a bulletin board.

     Alternate version: Type up the cards into a document and distribute to beginning teachers – and the rest of the faculty – in the fall.

- Encourage everyone to offer to share a practice, a strategy, or a piece of curriculum... something! A few teachers may think they have nothing special to offer; others may feel too busy. Building leaders who have visited everyone's classroom know from first hand observation what people's strengths are. Poke your head in the door some afternoon of those people who don't reply the first time. "Hey, Jane, would you be willing to show one of our novices how you set up literature groups some-time next fall?" The direct request may do the trick.

- During orientation in August, ask veteran teachers to share samples of student work with the beginning teachers that show a before and after snapshot of what students can be expected to produce at the beginning and end of the year. This means writing samples, lab reports, social studies essays, whatever is relevant to the class the beginning teacher will teach. The point is to give them a concrete idea of their incoming students' skills and what gains they should shoot for (and can expect) over the course of the year.

- Ask the PTO president to arrange for someone to deliver a rose to each beginning teacher at the end of the first day along with congratulations for having gotten over the first big hurdle.

- Before school or in the early weeks of school, arrange for neighborhood parties, dinners, coffees, whatever is appropriate, at school or in someone's home, so the beginning teachers can get to know community members and the parents of their

continued...

continued from previous page...

children. It is important to build bridges between beginning teachers and the community and to educate the beginning teacher about the community, its culture, where things are, the local history, and the conditions in which their children live. Some districts arrange a bus tour of the community for new teachers, which can be very helpful. We are also suggesting a deeper level of awareness of the city or town that helps new teachers meet community members. These events are hosted in the community rather than by the teachers. Their host role will come soon enough.

Component 6
District Wide Planning Process

The Stakeholders

The district plan for the induction of new teachers belongs to many people. These stakeholders must be represented in the process of conceptualizing and developing the plan.

Who are these stakeholders and why should they be involved?

Superintendents and Central Office Staff

Superintendents and other district administrators – and the school committee – are key players in demonstrating the district commitment to the plan. Their understanding of and support for the program are essential in ensuring that needed resources flow in its direction. Many districts establish the position of Program Coordinator to oversee the operations of the program. This may be a full time position in a very large district or a responsibility of a lead teacher or administrator in a small district.

Teachers Association

Enlightened associations want to be partners with superintendents and others in the administration to ensure that their new members receive the support and encouragement they will need to be effective and successful in the classroom. Professionalizing teaching requires joint ownership and accountability for the quality of teaching by unions and administrators. The teachers association should be represented on the planning and steering committee for the induction program.

Veteran Teachers

Because mentoring is a key component of most induction programs, it is important that veteran teachers play a role in shaping the decisions that will impact them and their colleagues.

Beginning Teachers

Teachers in their first few years in the school are a valuable source of information on the needs of new teachers and the realities of teaching in the first few years.

Principals

Principals are perhaps the key constituency in determining the success and effectiveness of an induction program.

Principal input – from every building in the district – into the macro and micro issues that are addressed by the plan is essential if the district is to develop a plan that will have the

continued...

continued from previous page...

support of the building leaders. The actions and attitudes of the school principal are key in modeling the kind of support for beginning teachers that is expected from all staff. Principals have opportunities to "walk their talk" through the actions they take such as scheduling that provides new and veteran teachers with common times for planning and "opposing" times for observations; the assignment of students to the new teachers' classroom; and the extracurricular expectations that are placed on new teachers. The decisions that principals make regarding the resources they uniquely control – such as time and scheduling – give powerful messages to other staff about what the principal values and supports.

The Planning Process

Most districts find that they can develop an initial draft of a plan in approximately two full days of intensive work. The goal of the planning committee is to develop a **framework** that outlines the district's approaches to the induction of beginning teachers. This framework should have sufficient flexibility in it to enable staff in individual buildings to make modifications that reflect the uniqueness of each school community. These modifications could relate to the process for the selection and matching of mentors and protégés, the frequency of mentor networking meetings, or other aspects of the plan.

Districts that have an informal support program in place for new teachers may want to start with a self-assessment of the strengths that exist in their schools. Appendix D provides a sample of a self-assessment tool that can be used to initiate the needs assessment process.

The planning process that the planning committee takes can be described as an **inverted pyramid**. The process starts by developing global understandings about the mission and goals of the induction program and, in a series of steps, narrows down its focus to the very concrete specifics of this district plan.

While there is great variation in the comprehensive induction plan that districts develop, they usually contain most or all of the elements described in the following pages.

A Mission or Vision Statement

The process of developing a **succinct** vision statement helps to confirm the group's mutual understanding about the program. It also provides a statement that can be used on brochures, handbooks, or in other materials that communicate about the program.

Samples:

> The purpose of the beginning teacher induction program is to provide professional and emotional support for the beginning teacher through mentoring and other complementary programs. The result of our program will be rapid growth of beginning teachers, increased professional collegiality among all staff, and enhanced student learning.

> The purpose of the XYZ Public Schools induction program for new teachers is to create a cadre of professionals who will enhance the quality of education for children. The program will result in building a positive, supportive, interactive learning environment for all educators and learners.

Although this process is critically important, it shouldn't take long to come up with a mission statement. Most of the planning time should be spent on the details of the plan itself.

Goals for the Induction Program

Induction programs are sometimes understood by teachers and administrators as programs that focus on the quality of teachers' lives in schools. While the existence of a congenial and collegial environment is important to the recruitment and retention of teachers, it is not the whole picture.

Induction programs are first and foremost about strengthening teaching and learning in the classroom. School districts are encouraged to develop goal statements that reflect the balance between outcomes for students (enhanced learning) and outcomes for new and veteran teachers (a school culture that supports collegial professional growth).

A Communications Plan

Many comprehensive induction programs are among the "best kept secrets" of the district. A communications plan helps the district to promote the program as a **valuable asset** of the district that is helping to attract and retain excellent teachers. It is a resource for administrators and others whose responsibility includes teacher recruitment, community awareness, and public relations.

A communications plan outlines:

WHAT folks in the community need to know about the district's induction program

WHO in the community should know about the program

HOW existing communications vehicles can be used to inform the community about the program

Roles and Responsibilities

The plan delineates the roles and responsibilities of the major players in a comprehensive induction program. These roles and responsibilities may vary from district to district. The descriptions outline the expectations that are held for teachers, administrators, union leaders, school committees, parents, and all others who have a stake in the success of beginning teachers.

In defining the roles and responsibilities, districts also describe the areas of responsibility that rest with central office administrators – the superintendent or curriculum directors – and the decisions that are made at the building level by principals and school staff.

For example:

- In some districts, all training for mentors and beginning teachers is coordinated at the central office; in others, staff development programs are organized at the building level.

- New teacher orientation programs may be coordinated at the district or building levels, or a combination of both.

- The process for selecting and matching mentors varies across districts and, sometimes, across buildings in a district.

Training and Networking

A comprehensive induction program includes workshops and courses for mentors and new teachers as well as training for administrators on their roles in supporting new teachers. Induction plans provide a multi-year outline of training and staff development that addresses the participants' needs for background information, research from the knowledge base on teaching, and strategies and techniques that contribute to strengthening teaching and learning.

Selection, Matching, and Other Specific Aspects of the Mentoring Program

The "nuts and bolts" of the mentor-pairing program are a key component of any plan. Decisions must be made regarding the process for selection and matching, the frequency of conferences and observations, the district policy on confidentiality, the roles and responsibilities of all players in the program, and other aspects of the operations of the mentor-pairing program.

Recognition and Appreciation of Mentors

The plan should explicitly describe the ways that mentors will be given recognition for the important work they are doing and the forms of reward that will be provided.

Piloting the Program

The size of the district sometimes determines whether a comprehensive induction program starts off in every school or only in a few schools. It also may determine whether all components of the plan are implemented at the same time or are phased into the district. The induction plan should describe a process for staging a full implementation of the program.

Program Assessment

A commitment to engage in on-going assessment of the effectiveness of the induction plan is essential to improvement and success. Plans should outline the information that will be gathered – and by whom – and the uses that will be made of this information. Mentors, protégés, and others can provide valuable insights that can strengthen even the best program.

Approval and Adoption of the Comprehensive Induction Program

In most districts, the group that develops the plan, sometimes called the Steering Committee, sends a final draft of the plan on to the Superintendent's Office (even if the superintendent has participated in the process) and to the Union Leadership, for their review. Once there is agreement on the specifics of the plan, it is sent to the School Committee (School Board). Local practice differs in whether the school committee reviews, accepts, or adopts the plan. In either case, the goal is to have school committee members aware of the plan, solidly behind its goals and approaches, understanding the financial and other resource implications of the plan, and willing to be "cheerleaders" for the program.

Component 7
On-Going Assessment

The purpose of on-going assessment of the program is to create a flow of information for monitoring and improving the program. Just as the primary purpose of assessment with students should be to improve instruction, the primary purpose of assessment is to improve the induction program. Without the information that is provided through assessment, efforts to adjust the program will be misguided or unconfirmed.

The assessment system should be designed at the same time as the overall planning process described above. We are separating it here in order to focus on the kinds of data to gather and to highlight the importance of directing the data to the appropriate decision makers.

Continuous Assessment

Evaluate the program, not the people.

An effective induction program takes its pulse often and in many different ways.

- Is the program useful for beginning teachers? Do they feel it is making a difference in their classroom teaching?

- What are the most useful forms of support for the second and third year teachers?

- Do the veteran teachers believe that the program is helping them to support the new teachers?

- How does the program contribute to improving student learning?

- How does the program support the professional growth of veteran teachers?

- What would be more useful approaches for making this program effective for new and veteran teachers?

Quantitative and Qualitative Measures

There are quantitative and qualitative ways to determine the impact that a comprehensive induction program is having on students and on staff.

At a very basic level, there are **quantitative measures**:

- How often are new and veteran teachers meeting in formal or informal conferences?

  – Are the interactions only formal meetings, or are the pairs engaging in more frequent informal conversations during the day or week?

  – Do the pairs have the time and access that enables informal as well as formal interaction to take place?

- What are the topics of the formal or informal conferences between mentors and mentees?

  – Is there a message for school administrators in the topics of the meetings? For example, it may become clear to the mentor that the mentee is getting conflicting messages about what the curriculum should be. This is information the mentor should bring forward. Does parent communication come up frequently? Are the teachers frequently seeking help with classroom management? Does stress management head the list of items discussed by new and veteran teachers? The answers to these questions may suggest that the administration needs to provide workshops, coaching, or other kinds of support for new teachers.

- In how many peer observations has the new teacher been involved?

  – Who has been observing whom? Do teachers have the time and coverage they need to engage in observations? Is there conferencing before and after the observations?

- How many workshops or professional development activities that are offered by the district have the mentor and the protégé attended? How do they rate these sessions in terms of their usefulness?

- What is the district's rate of retention of new teachers? How has it changed since before the program was instituted?

- What is the district's experience attracting candidates to its positions? What is the district's rate of hiring the teachers to whom it offers contracts? Has this changed since the program was instituted?

Qualitative approaches to evaluation give a fuller picture of the impact of the program and may offer suggestions on what the program is doing well or how the program could be strengthened. Qualitative assessment of the program also provides an indication of the impact that the program is having on new and veteran teachers and on the culture of the school or district.

- How do the beginning teacher and the mentor believe they have grown as a result of this program?

    – Which aspects of the beginning teacher's practice did he/she think were most influenced by the program?

    – What did the mentor find most/least satisfying about the program?

    – How could the program be improved?

        – What were the most useful aspects of the program? The least useful?

        – What suggestions do they have for the program?

        – What further support for the program should come from the district? The building principal?

Program evaluation is best done when it becomes a routine aspect of on-going activities.

- Use five or ten minutes during networking meetings of mentors or beginning teachers to engage in formal or informal assessment of how the program is going.

- Ask mentors, new teachers, superintendents, other administrators, union leaders, and relevant others to fill out surveys at intervals throughout the year (See Appendix E).

- Seek feedback from the teachers association on its assessment of the program. Information that teachers give to the association may differ in instructive ways from information gathered by the administration.

Careful and candid evaluation of the data generated by new and veteran teachers is critical. It provides information on aspects of the program to celebrate, ways in which the program can be strengthened, and suggestions for opportunities that can be realized. As districts respond to feedback on the induction program, they will motivate teachers and administrators to continue to provide thoughtful and constructive input.

Information from the evaluations should be shared with all constituencies who have a role in the success of beginning teachers. Using district and building newsletters, web sites, cable-tv, and the local media, disseminate the results of your data to teachers, administrators, the school committee, parents, potential candidates, and all others whose support and involvement are critical to the success of the program – or who potentially could benefit from it.

CHAPTER FOUR

Supervision and Evaluation of Beginning Teachers

In a comprehensive induction program, it is expected that the mentor is in a non-judgmental and non-evaluative relationship with the beginning teacher. Further, the mentor does not play a role in the evaluation of the beginning teacher and does not participate in decision making on the future employment of the new teacher.

It is the role of the administrator to support, supervise, and evaluate beginning teachers. The skills, knowledge, and beliefs that the administrator brings to this role can be vital to the success, professional growth, and retention of the new teacher. We include the supervision and evaluation of the beginning teacher in our comprehensive model because these functions are clearly part and parcel of the program of support that surrounds a new teacher and that can make the difference in the effectiveness of the new teacher.

Supervision and Evaluation Systems

Supervision and evaluation systems in school districts transmit the culture of the district. They send messages of trust or mistrust, support or "gotcha." They may take teaching seriously or produce a set of superficial inspection procedures that indirectly show disrespect for teachers.

Evaluation systems need to be able to deal with unsatisfactory teaching in ways that are fair, direct, and decisive; but that aspect of evaluation needs to be embedded in a larger system that emphasizes growth and professionalism. We have written elsewhere how to develop such evaluation systems (Saphier 1993; Platt et al 1999). Our partner organization, Research for Better Teaching, provides training on these topics. These books and courses describe how to create a comprehensive supervision and evaluation system so as to deliberately strengthen school culture and professional community. Beginning teachers, however, pose other issues for line supervisors like principals, assistant principals, and department chairs.

If you wrote down in a complete classroom observation of a beginning teacher everything you saw that needed improvement, you could easily overwhelm and discourage a beginning teacher. When it comes to the written part of supervision and evaluation, it is best in providing feedback to be selective and tackle doable chunks. Evaluation systems should be narrative, rather than checklist based, so that the evaluator can select and focus on the most important issues and not be pressed into completing elaborate, long rating lists too early in the year. In end of the year final evaluations, it is necessary for the evaluator to be honest in what is written. However, beware of overkill in the early months of the beginning teacher's experience.

Suggestions for Supervisors

Supervisors must be sensitive to the developmental needs of beginning teachers who are novices and look for ways to support them with their developmental issues. Typically (but not necessarily), beginning teachers have a lot to learn about classroom management, setting norms and routines, and dealing with disruptive behavior. At the same time, they may need support in planning lessons that are tightly aligned with curriculum objectives.

It may be that the first months of school are not the time to suggest that beginning teachers acquire skill with, for example, cooperative learning, even though cooperative learning could later play a role in lessening their discipline issues. As experienced teachers know, learning to do cooperative learning well takes a long time. Also, it doesn't lessen discipline problems if the problems are resulting from unclear expectations and erratic or no consequences for misbehavior.

If the beginning teacher has classroom management and lesson planning under control, then it may be appropriate to raise issues pertaining to variety – variety in instructional strategies, variety of types of learning experiences for students, or variety of explanatory devices (imagery, modeling thinking aloud, graphic organizers).

Mentors should always keep high on the agenda the beginning teachers' belief systems, especially their belief systems about students' capacity to learn. A supervisor can never neglect this issue, especially if there is evidence that the beginning teacher uses stereotypes in thinking about certain students or treats students differentially. However, the supervisor needs to bear in mind that a person over-whelmed with management issues is not likely to be able to reflect on their deepest beliefs about, for example, learnable intelligence.

If you pick up "beliefs about children" as an issue when classroom management problems erupt, "triage" the immediate problem and raise the beliefs issue at another time.

It is our strong belief that it is the responsibility of the supervisor to focus on behaviors that reflect the deepest beliefs about the capacity of all students to learn. It is in these early years of teaching that beginning teachers need to receive consistent and repeated messages that they should expect good thinking and effective effort from all their students. Beginning teachers need to be taught how to motivate all students and that they cannot accept the attitude that "some can and some can't learn and that's the way it is."

It is often said, "What's inspected is expected." It is not specific teaching behaviors but rather *habits of mind* that the supervisor must explicitly cultivate in the beginning teacher. These habits of mind are cultivated by asking certain questions over and over and consistently sharing any data that reflects the beginning teacher's beliefs about learners.

To be more specific, if a student isn't learning, a teacher needs to examine his/her own behavior, identify what can be changed, and examine the student's behavior. A supervisor may ask the new teacher who has a difficult student:

"Can you show me his latest work?"

"What exactly would be the next increment of progress for him?"

"What have you thought about doing differently?"

"Who might help you get some ideas?"

The supervisor's role – and the mentor's role – is to demonstrate that the beginning teacher must take responsibility for student outcomes. If the beginning teacher's attitude indicates low confidence in the student's ability, that attitude must be challenged.

"I'm told his brother was the same way."

"That's neither here nor there. He may be acting now like his brother did, but it's our responsibility to help him make different choices."

"He just doesn't have the ability to think in abstractions. He can't read and think about this material."

"He does, indeed, have trouble with fluent reading and the reading levels of these texts. But he can think as well as anyone if he has access to the information and if he is challenged and given time to think. We have to find a way to show our confidence in him and to overcome this input problem that walls him off from class discussions because of the reading."

The goal of supervision and mentoring for beginning teachers in their first three years is to take a developmental approach to supporting the new teacher to gain skills, attitudes and a repertoire of strategies. Consider the following progressive sequence of areas to which a supervisor may want the new teacher to pay attention:

• Classroom management

• Precision in lesson and unit planning for mastery thinking

• Good assessment with constant feedback to students

• Using a variety of instructional and classroom management strategies

• Adjustment of instruction for students' learning styles

- Advanced areas for teacher development

    – Classroom climate

    – Models of teaching including cooperative learning

    – In-depth knowledge of specific pedagogies

Overarching and running as a thread through all support of beginning teachers from the first day should be essential beliefs, particularly belief in the capacity of all students to do rigorous material at high standards – and the way this belief does or does not show up behaviorally in one's teaching.

CHAPTER FIVE

Maintaining and Sustaining Induction Programs

Administrators: A Key To Success

There is a high school principal – a strong advocate of induction programs for new teachers – who says:

> *"There are lots of things I can do to support the induction program in my building. But, there are many more things I can do to sabotage the program."*

The effectiveness and success of an induction program has a great deal to do with the support, nurturing, modeling, and enthusiasm of school and district administrators. Administrators set the standard for the level of commitment that is made to ensuring that new teachers are successful and that those who support new teachers are given the time and resources that are needed.

"Our principal met with all of the new teachers as a group – bi-weekly in the fall and monthly in the spring – to answer our questions, share information with us, and engage us in discussions about our experiences as new teachers."

Beginning Teacher

"My principal was great about covering my classroom a few times for 5 or 10 minutes so that I could watch my mentor or another teacher using a strategy I wanted to understand better."

Beginning Teacher

"Our superintendent made it clear that supporting our new teachers was a priority for her. Mentors were given time to meet with the new teachers – both for conferences and for observing. We also met with the principal three times during the year to discuss how the program was going and ways that the school could be more supportive of new teachers."

Veteran Mentor Teacher

A School and District Wide Culture that Values and Promotes the On-going Professional Growth of All Staff

Superintendents, principals, and other administrators have numerous opportunities daily to demonstrate their priorities through:

- The issues and programs to which they give their attention
- The visible, personal support they provide to programs and activities
- The areas in which they proclaim their "outrage"
- The topics to which they give priority at their meetings

Administrators' actions speak in volumes that are louder than their words. Principals and other administrators who "walk the talk" by facilitating meetings and interactions between new teachers and their mentors will find that others pick up the message and act similarly.

Program Coordinators and Steering Committees: Institutional Structures that Support the Program

As districts hire increasing numbers of new teachers, it becomes critical that they incorporate the support of new teachers into their organizational structure.

Most districts designate an administrator or teacher as the program coordinator who oversees the implementation of the program. The coordinator often has a multi-faceted role that includes:

• Collaborating with others to design and implement the district orientation program for new teachers

• Arranging for training activities for mentors and for beginning teachers that are appropriate to their developmental levels during their first three years

• Convening new teachers and mentors for informational and socializing meetings during the year

• Overseeing the collection of data on the induction program

• Reporting to the superintendent, other central office administrators, and the school committee on the program's successes and weaknesses

• Providing mediation, and reassignment if needed, for beginning teacher-mentor pairs

Coordinators are wise to seek the support of a steering committee that can serve as additional "eyes and ears" of the program in the schools. Some steering committees are composed of a representative from each building while others include new and veteran teachers, building administrators and central office staff, and teacher union representatives. Steering committees help to monitor the development of programs, recommend workshop topics for new and veteran teachers, and encourage participation in the program.

Roadblocks for Induction Programs

Respect the Fragility of the Program

When induction programs lose the support and respect of the staff, it is often for one of two reasons:

Confidentiality. There must be no breaches in the assumption of confidentiality for the new teacher or the mentor.

When principals seek to get information on new teachers from their mentors, that is a breach of confidentiality. Similarly, when principals or other supervisors seek to give messages to new teachers through their mentors, that is a breach of confidentiality.

In either case, if beginning teachers or their mentors sense in any way that the confidentiality of their relationship is endangered, the induction program will run into trouble. Principals and other administrators – as well as other teachers in the building, need to understand that the new teachers are valued professionals in the building and that they are to be treated the same as other professionals in the school. Principals or supervisors must rely on their own first-hand sources of information on the professional performance of new teachers – and not on data from mentors. Principals also should not view mentors as a conduit of information to beginning teachers.

> *Equity. There must be equality in all decisions made regarding the forms of support that are provided for beginning teachers.*

If beginning teachers come to believe that the induction program represents an effort at "remediation" for new teachers, few new teachers will be willing to participate in the program.

Sometimes, a district is not able to provide a mentor for all of its new teachers – or to provide new teacher workshops for everyone. In these cases, districts are advised to find criteria that will ensure that there is no tinge of remediation or any other form of stigma associated with their decision-making. When there are more new teachers than mentors, for example, find a rationale for making assignments, such as making mentor pairings only for novice teachers and not those who are new to the district. If not all new teachers can be accommodated in workshops, make workshops voluntary or establish criteria for who has the highest priority for participating, such as novice teachers in their first and second years of practice.

Respect the Program and the Participating Teachers

Induction programs are complex and sensitive initiatives in any school district. They ask highly valued teachers to share their expertise and accumulated wisdom with the newest members of the school community. Induction programs provide these educational role models with opportunities to carry forward into the future the treasury of knowledge, attitudes, and beliefs that have sustained them through their careers.

Mentors will question themselves, if not school administrators, about how truly they are valued if they are not given the time they need to do this important job effectively. If the most valuable asset of any school is its teachers – and surely it is! – then the administration of that school will be wise to ensure that it demonstrates its respect and appreciation for all of its staff – including its most accomplished members as they support the newcomers.

An induction program provides opportunities for school leaders to demonstrate their commitment to staff development and growth in the school community. If the induction program is perceived by staff as a way for administrators to shift their responsibilities to the mentor teachers, they will not achieve their potential and they will lower morale in the schools. If they are an extension of the school's commitment to continued growth and life-long learning and sharing, they will reinforce the culture and environment of the school and multiply the benefits for teachers and students.

Unexpected Benefits

A well-designed induction program is essentially excellent staff development.

"The best part of being a mentor was having the opportunity to get new ideas from my beginning teacher. Sometimes it seemed that I learned as much from her as I was able to share with her."

Veteran Mentor Teacher

"My mentor and I took a course on teaching in a standards-based classroom that was helpful in giving us a way to talk with each other about our teaching. He told me that our discussions were as useful to him as I felt they were to me."

Beginning Teacher

An effective comprehensive induction program is based on the sharing of the knowledge base on teaching among new and veteran teachers. Surveys of new and veteran teachers demonstrate that both groups of educators find that the training that is incorporated into these programs benefits both the new and the veteran teachers.

The activities of mentoring involve the collegial behaviors that were identified by Judith Warren Little and Susan Rosenholtz (1982) as key to strengthening classroom practice.

Collegiality

A high frequency of teachers **TALKING WITH EACH OTHER ABOUT TEACHING**.

A high frequency of teachers **OBSERVING EACH OTHER**.

A high frequency of teachers **PLANNING, MAKING, AND EVALUATING CURRICULUM MATERIALS TOGETHER**.

A high frequency of teachers **TEACHING EACH OTHER** about the practice of teaching.

A high frequency of teachers **ASKING FOR AND WILLING TO PROVIDE** one another with **ASSISTANCE**.

– Judith Warren Little/ Susan Rosenholtz

When new and veteran teachers engage in "teacher talk," spend time in each other's classrooms, and in other ways support each other's teaching and learning, children benefit from the higher level of teaching that takes place in their classrooms.

Subsequent research continues to indicate that professional development that is embedded in the school – on the job – is the most effective approach for impacting classroom practice and student achievement. Newmann, Wehlage (1995), and others have found that students whose teachers have developed a true professional community have gains that are significant statistically and large in magnitude compared to similar students in schools in which teachers are not engaged in collaborative learning. Based on this research, it is reasonable to assume that new teachers who have on-going conversations with their mentors aimed at strengthening their practice and supporting their experimentation with new approaches and techniques, are more likely to engage their students in learning and thinking that results in higher student achievement.

Effective induction programs inherently work to transform the culture of a school.

Induction programs that pair new and veteran teachers build a comfort zone for practicing collegial behaviors, especially the behavior which many teachers find the most difficult – classroom observations. Veteran teachers report that they are more comfortable being observed teaching by a beginning teacher than by another veteran colleague – and that the comfort level increases as they gain experience.

If there are six new teachers in a school this year and each is paired with a mentor with whom they engage in reciprocal observations, the school now has 12 teachers who are expanding their ability to engage in collegial practice. If next year, another six new teachers and six mentors are paired for similar practice, the number obviously expands. After three or four years, it may be that every teacher in the school has participated in collegial conferencing and observing with a new or veteran colleague. The multiplier effect can be powerful – especially if teachers are given training, time, and support for these collegial interactions.

"All of the beginning teachers in the school were asked to identify practices they would like to observe in another teacher's classroom, such as the use of graphic organizers, a particular cooperative learning structure, or a use for PowerPoint presentations. Some of my colleagues and I asked if we could also have a chance to do some of these observations. Taking up this suggestion, the principal sent around a survey asking all teachers to identify two practices they would like to observe in another classroom and two practices they would be pleased to demonstrate to others. We used a faculty meeting to discuss how we would maximize the benefits of these observations by linking them to pre and post observation conversations on the practices being observed. These focused observations have changed many attitudes in our school! It is now common practice for teachers to share, observe, and learn from each other on a regular basis. As a result, I think we all are feeling that we are better teachers – and that our children are getting better teaching from us."

Veteran Teacher

As veteran teachers work to support new teachers, a sometimes unexpected and powerful benefit is the change that happens in the culture of the whole school. All teachers become more willing to experiment and to engage in open and honest communication about their practice.

CHAPTER SIX
Conclusion

Every Child Deserves an Expert Teacher

...a teacher who can think and problem-solve, based on an ever growing base of professional knowledge

...a teacher who knows and cares about them personally

...a teacher who works in a school district that knows and cares about every beginning teacher's growth toward real expertise

> *"Every child deserves an expert teacher."*

We not only support this claim about the need for expert teachers, but believe it should be an urgent national policy. A democracy that claims every citizen can rise on his or her merit owes its children the chance to develop their minds and their possibilities. This opportunity does not take place for all youngsters, especially economically disadvantaged youngsters whose education is hampered by poor or mediocre teaching. Further, we know that the cumulative effect of several poor teachers in a row creates damage that is extremely difficult to overcome later (Sanders, 1995).

What, then, is expertise in teaching and how does one acquire it?

Expert teachers have knowledge, skills, and beliefs that create a particular form of professionalism. Shulman (1986) and Berliner (1987) found that compared to novices, experts recognized patterns of behavior in interpreting complex classroom events. Dreyfus (1986) and Benner (2000) found that as experts move away from rule governed behavior, which served them well as novices, they exercise more decision making acumen and deliberate choice making from their ever increasing repertoires to match the current needs of curriculum, situations, and children. Expert teachers are decision makers whose decisions are based on ever more complex schema of variables.

Bereiter and Scardamalia, in the little known *Surpassing Ourselves – An Inquiry into the Nature and Implications of Expertise* (1993), argue that expertise includes – but is more than – exercising decisions based on a broad repertoire of possibilities. They claim expertise is a process in which individuals continually engage. The presence and cultivation of the following attributes characterizes an expert teacher:

- Reinvestment in learning

- Seeking out ever more difficult problems one had not seen or tackled before

- Tackling more complex representations of recurrent problems

A teacher who assembles a constellation of strategies and successfully overcomes the reading problems of several of her students now tackles the issue of critical reading with the same children. A teacher who overcomes discipline problems and becomes an accomplished classroom manager sees and tackles the available issue of building a supportive, helpful community among the students. It is an "available issue" to her because she is an inquirer, a questioner, and a professional who is always pressing her own growing edge and looking for and defining the next problem that will push her practice further. That is what real experts do.

We endorse this view of expertise. Comprehensive induction programs are just part of what should be a seamless continuum of experiences that lead a person toward becoming an expert teacher. To do so, induction must embody a comprehensive map of teaching knowledge that will assist in perceiving and then defining the next level of problem-solving for leading edge teachers. That is why we have adopted a view of professional knowledge that is based on repertoire and matching rather than lists of effective behaviors to be learned. It is also why we have stressed the beliefs and attitudes about learning and about children that must be built into mentor training, beginning teacher courses, and the design of the induction program itself.

Let us use the knowledge we have and mobilize the resources at our disposal to give quality teaching to our children. Let us give them a comprehensive induction system that will grow expert teachers.

APPENDICES

APPENDICES

APPENDIX A

Sample Plan for
a Comprehensive Induction
Program

IDEALTOWN Public Schools Plan
for the Comprehensive Induction of New Teachers

The Idealtown Public Schools are committed to the success of all members of our school community – students and teachers. In order to support the large number of new teachers we are bringing into our schools, we have developed this comprehensive induction program that engages new and veteran teachers in collegial, professional growth.

Mission Statement

for the Idealtown Public Schools Comprehensive Induction Program

The purpose of the Idealtown Public Schools induction program is to provide a supportive professional community for teachers who are new to our school district. As a result of this program, we will enhance the collegial environment in our schools and facilitate on-going professional growth for new and veteran teachers that results in effective teaching and enhanced student learning.

Induction Program Goals

1. *To integrate new teachers into the culture and climate of our schools and our school district*

2. *To assist beginning teachers to manage the challenges that are common to all new teachers*

3. *To enhance new and veteran teachers' personal and professional development through reflection on their practice and on student learning*

4. *To retain highly qualified teachers in our schools*

Acknowledgements

The Idealtown Public Schools appreciate the involvement of the following individuals in the development of this Plan:

Dr. Larry Finn   Superintendent, Idealtown Public Schools

Dr. Steven Brooks   Director of Curriculum

Ms. Margie Sanchez   Principal, Goldenrod School

Mr. Juan Martinez   Principal, Evergreen School

Ms. Genevieve Pierce   Teacher, Science, IHS
                               Idealtown Teachers Association Representative

Mr. Kevin Ellis   Teacher, Woodland Elementary School

Ms. Stephanie Santos   Teacher, Evergreen Elementary School

Ms. Shelby Grace   Teacher, Idealtown Middle School

Mr. Joel Green   Teacher, Idealtown High School

Ms. Amanda Ansonia   Teacher, Idealtown Middle School

We would like to express our appreciation to Tanya Thomas for her assistance in facilitating the process that resulted in the development of this plan.

Other Options that Idealtown might have chosen...

- *Convene a steering committee to review the district's current program for supporting new teachers.*
- *Drawing on the model offered in this booklet, identify components of the existing program that need to be strengthened or added.*
- *Draft a proposed induction plan that is reviewed by the administration and the teachers union. Make changes as appropriate and present the plan to the school committee and the community.*

Communication Plan

The Idealtown Public Schools recognize that the Comprehensive Induction Program is a valuable asset of our school district. It helps to implement our district goal of ensuring that our schools provide a highly professional environment in which effective approaches to teaching and learning guide all work for students and teachers. It also helps to ensure that Idealtown is able to attract and retain the strongest teachers to teach the children in our schools.

In order to ensure that the school community is aware of the benefits and operations of the induction program, a communications plan has been developed to expand community awareness of the program. This plan includes three components:

WHO should know about our comprehensive induction program?

- Teachers and other staff in our schools
- Parents and parent organizations
- School councils and advisory groups
- School administrators
- Superintendent and central office staff
- School committee
- Businesses in town, including realtors
- Local media
- Candidates for teaching positions
- Area colleges and universities
- The Department of Education
- Recently retired teachers who may want to help with the mentoring program

continued...

WHAT *should they know about our comprehensive induction program?*

- The research and rationale for an induction program
- The benefits of the program for students and teachers
- The cost benefits for the district
- The demographics of teachers in Idealtown – and the numbers of new teachers we will be hiring
- The expectations for mentors and their mentees
- How the program works: time expectations; information sharing; personal and professional support
- The workshops and other training in which new and veteran teachers will participate
- The resources needed: time, training, coordination, and funding

WHAT *vehicles should be used to inform the school community and the larger community about the program?*

- District newsletters
- District brochures
- District cable-tv program
- District web site
- Presentations at school committee meetings
- Principals' newsletters
- Back-to-school nights and other school events
- Special features in the local media

ROLES AND RESPONSIBILITIES

of Key Players in
the Idealtown Public Schools
Induction Program

Role of the Beginning Teacher

To become knowledgeable about and to participate in the Idealtown Public Schools Induction Program

To welcome daily, informal support from mentors

To meet with mentor for a total of approximately 2-3 hours per week in formal and informal interactions

To keep a log of weekly meetings and to maintain a reflective journal

To be open to feedback and the practice of reflective teaching

To maintain the confidentiality of the mentor-mentee relationship

To develop a professional development plan and strive to address three specific professional goals

To meet and conference regularly with other new teachers

To be open, candid and willing to share and try new ideas

To be an active listener and willing to "try again"

To participate in the district's on-going assessment of the induction program

Role of the Mentor Teacher

To become knowledgeable about and to participate in the Idealtown Public Schools Induction Program

To attend training on the roles and responsibilities of mentors

To recognize that mentoring is an on-going commitment

To meet with the beginning teacher for 2-3 hours weekly in formal and informal interactions to determine his/her needs, offer personal and emotional support and encouragement, and provide information and guidance about school practices and policies, curriculum, classroom management, and other related issues

To be open to feedback and the practice of reflective teaching

To be willing to be observed by the beginning teacher

To be willing to observe and provide constructive feedback to the beginning teacher

To facilitate resource acquisition and open communication among the new teacher, other teachers, the principal, and other administrators

To offer support through active listening and by sharing experiences

To be a coach, a buddy, and to model professionalism

To maintain professional respect and confidentiality around the mentoring relationship

To attend support and professional development meetings related to the induction program

To participate in all phases of an on-going assessment of the induction program

Role of Principals

To become knowledgeable about the induction program and to factor the needs of the program into decisions made at the school such as scheduling, class assignments, etc.

To respect the confidentiality of the mentor-new teacher relationship

To inform prospective teachers about the induction program and its requirements

To support and encourage eligible staff members to participate in the mentoring program

To attend and participate in the induction program training for administrators

To inform faculty and parents about the program and its benefits

To coordinate an orientation program for new teachers and other hospitality events for new teachers

To select mentors for new teachers from a pool of veteran teachers who have been trained as mentors

To make the matches between mentors and new teachers taking into consideration grade level, subject matter, proximity, and personal style

To build an active support team around each beginning teacher

To provide and protect mentor-mentee time for planning, observing and conferencing

To serve as a mediator where necessary

To model professionalism and support for the program

To participate in all phases of an on-going assessment of the induction program

Role of the ITA

(Idealtown Teachers Association)

To participate as a partner in the development and refinement of the Idealtown Comprehensive Induction Plan and Program

To become knowledgeable about the program and its components and to provide input into its on-going improvement

To demonstrate union support for the induction program

To inform beginning teachers about ITA opportunities

To inform veteran teachers about the opportunity for mentoring and mentor training

To take a leadership role in advocating for new teachers within the Idealtown Public Schools

To support the incorporation of language into the contract that supports new teachers and their mentors

To provide sustained, positive, informal communications about the induction program

To recognize the intangible benefits of a mentoring program such as increased community support and understanding of the education profession

To participate in all phases of an on-going assessment of the induction program

Role of the Superintendent and Central Office

To become knowledgeable about the induction program and its components and provide input into its on-going improvement

To participate in the Idealtown Public Schools Induction Program through activities such as the Orientation Program

To provide funding to support the program

To provide for beginning teachers a packet of information about the community and the school district

To serve as a "cheerleader" for the program

To provide visible staff support and to promote the goals of the program

To support the need for training, time for mentors and mentees to meet, and other resources necessary for an effective program

To actively communicate with the administrative team regarding the program's progress and impact

To act as a liaison between the school committee and the community for the program

To serve as an advocate of the induction program to the wider community

To create a climate that encourages on-going assessment and to support changes as necessary

To model the intrinsic belief that a strong induction program will have a significant positive impact on students

To assess effectiveness of the program through a cost benefit analysis including teacher retention and student achievement data

Role of the School Committee

To welcome new teachers and demonstrate support for the program during the Idealtown Public School's orientation program

To provide a liaison for the induction program steering committee

To provide financial support for the program

To adopt a policy that ensures that all beginning teachers will have a mentor and training

To act as community "cheerleaders" supporting the program as inherently good for children and the school community

To facilitate contractual negotiations that will support the induction program

To maintain an open and supportive dialogue with members of the community, parents, and teachers

To participate in all phases of an on-going assessment of the induction program

To assess effectiveness of the program through a cost benefit analysis including teacher retention and student achievement data

Role of the Other Members of the School Faculty

To be welcoming and supportive of new faculty

To attend a workshop to learn about the induction program

To provide information about formal and informal policies, procedures and resources to beginning teachers

To encourage and support new teachers by:
- being friendly
- sharing supplies
- sharing curriculum ideas
- respecting confidentiality
- sharing knowledge, skills and strategies

To provide a positive school climate that contributes to the success of all adults and students

To read communications (newsletters, union information, newspaper articles, etc...) about the program

To share individual challenges with new teachers so they know they aren't alone

To consider being a mentor in future years

Role of the Program Coordinator

To become knowledgeable about the program and its components and provide input into its on-going improvement

To participate in the planning of the new teacher orientation

To encourage teachers to participate as mentors

To plan monthly meetings on key topics for beginning teachers or mentors

To coordinate and oversee professional development programs for beginning teachers, mentors, and administrators

To chair meetings of the Induction Program Steering Committee

To oversee and facilitate the monitoring and implementation of the district induction plan

To develop an annual program review that is based on data from the program and that is shared with the Program Steering Committee

To mediate mentor-protégé pairings if necessary

To apply for grants for induction programs and seek other sources of funding to supplement the line item in the budget

To direct the evaluation of the program throughout the year

To develop periodic reports on the program for the superintendent and the school committee

Governance of the Program

The program coordinator position carries with it a stipend and the reduction of 1/5 teaching load.

An Induction Program Steering Committee, composed of the program coordinator, superintendent or assistant superintendent, two principals, three veteran teachers and two second year teachers, will provide guidance and feedback to the program coordinator.

The Program Steering Committee will meet at least once a year for a program review that is based on data collected by the program coordinator. Following this review by the steering committee, a report will be developed by the program coordinator and sent to the superintendent.

Other Options that Idealtown might have chosen...

In smaller districts, the responsibility of coordinating the induction program is given to an assistant superintendent or a school principal. In large districts, the responsibility may need to become a full time position.

The committee that develops the plan for the induction program may become the nucleus of the steering committee. The individuals who comprise the planning committee are often the same individuals who are interested in the on-going success of the program.

Who is a New Teacher in Idealtown?

In the Idealtown Public Schools, a new teacher is any teacher who is new to the profession or new to the Idealtown Public Schools.

New teachers are paired with a mentor for one year.

Other Options that may be considered...

A new teacher might be defined as any teacher who is new to the district or new to a grade level or content area.

Teachers who are new to the profession or new to the district could be paired with a mentor for one to three years, with reduced requirements for the number of meetings that are held in each successive year.

Teachers who are new to the profession or new to the district could be paired with a different teacher for each of the three years of the mentor pairing program in order to provide them with a range of models of teaching.

Training and Networking for New Teachers

Training

New teachers in the Idealtown Public Schools are highly encouraged to participate in the Teachers[21] *Beginning Teacher Institute*, a 36-hour course which carries with it 4 optional graduate credits. This course is designed specifically to address the needs of new teachers in their first or second year of practice.

This course will be given once during the year, starting in August. Two full days of the course will take place in August. The additional 24 hours of the course will take place in 3 hour sessions after school and 6 hour sessions on occasional Saturdays. An announcement of this course will be given to all new teachers upon their being hired into the district.

New teachers will also be expected to participate in other professional development offered by the district or their school that addresses learning goals for the school.

Teachers in their second and third years of practice will be expected to focus their training on content areas, content-specific pedagogy, and student assessment.

New Teacher Meetings

New teachers will be expected to meet monthly as a group with the induction coordinator or his/her designee for the sharing of information, addressing of issues, and to provide feedback on the induction program.

Beginning Teacher Network

A *Beginning Teacher Network* will be convened by a highly qualified lead teacher from within the district for the purpose of providing a small group of 4 – 6 new teachers with a supportive environment for addressing issues related to their classroom practice and professional relationships. This lead teacher will be identified according to criteria that have been included in the teachers' contract that was ratified in 1999.

The Network meets 10 times in one-hour sessions during the school year. A brochure describing this program is available from the program coordinator.

Criteria and Expectations for Mentors in Idealtown

District-wide minimum criteria and expectations for mentors have been established for the Idealtown Public Schools Induction Program.

Criteria for Mentors:

- Teachers with professional status and at least 3 years of experience
- Skillful communicators who can adapt to different communication styles
- Teachers who are current on and implement the best educational practice and who are committed to constant learning about the art and craft of teaching
- Teachers who are committed to collegial practices and experimentation
- Teachers with a proven track record for successful classroom practice
- Teachers with a track record for persevering and building confidence with resistant students
- Teachers who have completed a program of study in mentoring and supporting new teachers

Other Options Idealtown could have considered......

- *Able to commit the time that is required*
- *Demonstrates a broad repertoire of teaching skills and an understanding of the district's standards and expectations*
- *Possesses personal skills such as enthusiasm, commitment to teaching, and a demonstrated ability to work with peers*
- *Exhibits knowledge of and skills with conferencing and observation*
- *Agrees to participate in a training program for mentors*
- *Flexible and organized*
- *Possesses a sense of humor*
- *Demonstrates a commitment to personal professional development and an openness to new ideas and methodology*

Expectations for Mentors

- Mentor will be available approximately 3 hours per week to work with the new teacher

- Mentor will complete, in the first year, a 36-hour course in mentor skill training. The first 12 hours of this course will be completed prior to starting the mentoring relationship. In the second year, mentors will complete an additional 36 hours of advanced mentor training.

- Mentor will observe new teacher or otherwise be present in new teacher's classroom at least once weekly.

- Mentors will be relieved of certain duties and meetings to provide them with time to engage in the mentoring relationship.

- Mentors will meet two times a year as a group with the principal and program coordinator for problem-solving and to assess the effectiveness of the program.

- Mentor and mentee will maintain logs that document their time together for purposes of accountability. These logs will also include a one-word description of the topics discussed (classroom management; parent conferences; lesson planning; etc.).

Services for Mentors

Training

All mentors are required to take the Mentoring New Teachers 36-hour course during the first year that they are a mentor. The first 12 hours of the course should be taken prior to starting the mentoring relationship. In the second year, mentors will complete an additional 36 hours of Advanced Mentor Training.

Networking

All mentors will be expected to meet as a group with the principal and program coordinator two times during the year to share issues related to mentoring, engage in joint problem-solving, and provide feedback on the induction program.

Services for Administrators

All central office and building administrators will participate in an institute on comprehensive induction that provides information on the roles, responsibilities, and expectations of stakeholders in induction programs.

Administrators will also participate in institutes that address the role of the supervisor in supporting, supervising, and evaluating beginning teachers. These institutes will also focus administrators on building a growth-oriented culture in their schools.

Program Evaluation

The district will engage in on-going assessment of the program through the following vehicles:

Quantitative Data

The following data will be gathered on the program:

- Number of new teachers and mentors participating
- Logs that document the time and the focus of their conferences and observations
- Retention statistics on new and veteran teachers
- Professional development programs in which the new teacher participated
- Professional development programs in which the mentor participated
- Number of individuals who were offered contracts and who accepted these contracts

Qualitative Data

The district and individual schools will use a variety of approaches for collecting qualitative data on the program:

- Mid-year and end of year attitudinal surveys
- Summative questionnaires after training and networking events
- Formal and informal data gathering from participants about the aspects of their practice that were impacted by the program
- Formal and informal data gathering on improving the program
- Implementation of the state Department of Education induction program survey at the end of the year

Data gathered on the program will be documented and reported to the superintendent, the school board, and the school community through the superintendent's newsletter. Data will be reviewed by the Induction Program Steering Committee. Recommendations and suggestions are welcome and will be considered for implementation into the program.

SAMPLE FORMS

for the Idealtown Public Schools

SAMPLE A

Idealtown Public Schools

The Mentoring Program

ALL teachers are invited to participate in the induction program for new teachers.

How do YOU get started?

1. Attend an orientation meeting that explains the program. These programs will be held in the Spring of each year. (A flyer announcing the program is attached to this Plan.)

2. Complete the district application for mentoring that is attached to this Plan.

3. To become a mentor, you must participate in training. Enroll for a 36-hour, 4 graduate credit course on Mentoring New Teachers. See your principal for details.

4. The matching of mentors with new teachers will be done by building principals.

5. The Steering Committee, composed of building principals, a union representative, the mentor coordinator, and new and veteran teachers, will provide leadership and direction to the program. This committee will also coordinate training and networking programs for beginning teachers and mentors.

6. The district seeks to establish a "mentor pool" that will give us a source of trained mentors who will be able to support the large number of new teachers – at all grade levels – that we expect in the next 5 years.

Other Approaches that could be used:

Many administrators find that asking specific teachers to apply to become mentors is a useful and productive approach. Some teachers who would be excellent mentors do not recognize this potential in themselves or need some encouragement to step forward.

All interested teachers can be invited to participate in the orientation to mentoring with the understanding that:
1. *not all of them will be selected to be mentors*
2. *participation does not obligate them to become mentors*

If application procedures do not produce sufficient mentor candidates, principals will select the veteran teachers whom they would like to be mentors of the new teachers. These selections will be based in part on their knowledge of the teachers whom they have hired for the new school year as well as the criteria of grade level, content area, and proximity in the building. Principals will work to arrange the mentor-mentee teachers' schedules so as to provide common meeting time and opposing times for classroom observations.

SAMPLE B

Idealtown Public Schools

Announcing the Idealtown Public Schools Mentor Program for New Teachers

Join your colleagues for an informational meeting on becoming a mentor teacher
DATE – TIME
LOCATION

Next year, 41 new teachers will be joining our staff. Because this is a record number of new teachers for any one year – and we can anticipate that we will be hiring numbers of new teachers in each of the next 3-5 years, the district has developed a Comprehensive Induction Program to support teachers new to Idealtown.

We would like YOU to consider being a mentor to a new teacher.
Mentoring is a wonderful way for you to share your wisdom and expertise, learn new ideas and strategies from a new teacher, and give back to your profession.

Criteria for Mentor Teachers
- Professional status and at least 3 years of experience
- Skillful communicators who can adapt to different communication styles
- Current on and implement the best educational practice; committed to constant learning about the art and craft of teaching
- Committed to collegial practices and experimentation
- A proven track record for successful classroom practice
- Evidence of persevering and building confidence with resistant students
- Completion of a program of study in mentoring and supporting new teachers

Mentor Matching
Mentors will be matched with new teachers based on grade level, content area, and proximity in their buildings.

Requirements
- Willingness to be available to a beginning teacher for a total of approximately 2-3 hours per week
- Willingness to observe a beginning teacher 3 times and to be observed 3 times, with accompanying pre and post conferences

Stipend: $ plus   Professional Development Points

RSVP:

SAMPLE C
Idealtown Public Schools

Mentor Application and Matching Form

Part A: Mentor Teacher Application

I am interested in being considered for the position of a Mentor Teacher in the Comprehensive Induction Program. I understand that the role of a mentor is critical to the success of a novice teacher and ultimately key to the success of the children of Idealtown.

Name: _____

1. What specific personal and professional qualities would you bring to mentoring a new teacher?

   _____

   _____

   _____

   _____

   _____

   _____

   _____

2. How are you keeping current with your own professional development? What steps are you taking to be up-to-date on issues of curriculum and assessment?

   _____

   _____

   _____

   _____

   _____

   _____

   _____

continued...

3. What do you hope to gain from becoming a mentor?

_____
_____
_____
_____
_____
_____
_____

Signature: _____ **Date:** _____

Part B: For Office Use Only

Selection Committee's comments:

_____
_____
_____
_____
_____
_____
_____

Part C: Principal's Mentor – New Teacher Match

School: _____
Principal's Name: _____

I have selected **(name of mentor)** _____
who currently holds the position of **(grade and subject)** _____
to serve as a mentor teacher to **(name of new teacher)** _____
who has been appointed to the position of **(grade and subject)** _____

Principal's Signature: _____ **Date:** _____

SAMPLE D

Idealtown Public Schools

Application for the Position of Mentor of a New Teacher

Name: _____

School: _____

Department/Grade: _____

Years in the Idealtown Public Schools: _____

Areas of Certification: _____

_____

Please write a statement about your interest in becoming a mentor and how you think you can assist a first year teacher in our district.

_____

_____

_____

_____

_____

_____

_____

I understand that I will be required to participate in a 36-hour mentor training course if I am chosen as a mentor. The first 12 hours must be completed before my work as a mentor begins.

Signature: _____ **Date:** _____

APPENDIX B

Ideas for Providing Reward and Recognition

Ideas for Rewards and Recognition

- Stipends
- Professional Development Points
- *Time* to work with beginning teachers
  - Extra preparation periods
  - Release from duties
  - Reduced teaching load
- Professional development opportunities
- Credit mentor experience toward step/lane advancement
- Increased classroom supply budget
- Training on being a mentor
- Skill training for working with protégés
- Recognition ceremonies
- Articles spotlighting mentors
- Mentor support groups
- Opportunities to take courses
- Vouchers
- Tuition reimbursement

Intrinsic rewards

- Opportunity to help a beginning teacher
- Opportunity to improve own teaching

Suggested guidelines for teachers' contracts: Include funds for providing stipends to mentor teachers. Most districts do not include stipends for beginning teachers.

APPENDIX C

Sample School Schedule and Calendar of Events

Sample School Schedule and Calender of Events

August 28	Orientation for new teachers
August 29	New Teacher Meeting and Reception
September 5	First day of school
September 26	Back to School Night
October 5	Parents' Picnic
October 24	Parent Conferences start
October 26	First marking period ends
	Report cards due in the office on October 31
November 6	Math Night at school
November 21	Thanksgiving vacation
	Vacation starts at noon on Wednesday
December 19	Holiday celebration for parents and students
December 23	Holiday Vacation starts
January 2	Holiday Vacation ends
January 18	Second Marking Period ends
	Report cards due in the office on January 23
February 7	Science Night at school
February 17	Winter Vacation starts
February 24	Winter Vacation ends
March 29	Third marking period ends
	Report cards due in the office on April 3
April 13	Spring Vacation starts
April 21	Spring Vacation ends
May 3	State testing starts
May 24	Portfolio celebrations begin
June 14	Fourth marking period ends
	Report cards due in the office on June 19
June 21	Last day of school (if no snow days)

APPENDIX D

Self-Assessment Tool for School Districts

Self-Assessment Tool for School Districts

This survey is designed to give union and school leaders an opportunity to reflect on the areas in which their district is incorporating the elements of a comprehensive induction program.

Self-Assessment Tool for School Districts

Place an "X" in the box that is appropriate for each item.	YES	NO	Partially
District-wide Planning Process			
Has our district engaged a broadly based group of teachers and administrators in the process of developing a plan for the district's induction program that includes the teachers union and the school administration?			
Does a district-wide steering committee monitor the implementation of the program and use feedback to adjust and improve it?			
Criteria-based Selection and Matching of Mentors			
Does our district have criteria or qualifications for the selection of mentors?			
Are mentors selected based on the criteria that have been established by the district (if they exist)?			
Does our district have criteria for the matching of mentors and protégés?			
Are the matches between mentors and protégés made based on criteria established by the district?			
Mentor Services			
Do mentors receive training in the skills of providing positive feedback and differential conferencing in advance of being paired with beginning teachers?			
Do mentors receive training in the skills of providing support in the areas of curriculum and instruction for beginning teachers?			
Is there a specified expectation regarding the frequency of interactions (conferences; observations) between the mentor and the protégé?			

continued...

Place an "X" in the box that is appropriate for each item.	YES	NO	Partially
Beginning Teacher Services			
Do the beginning teachers in the district participate in workshops (on topics such as classroom management, building a classroom culture, working with families, etc.) that are specifically tailored to the needs of beginning teachers?			
Are beginning teachers brought together in networking groups regularly during the year?			
Are beginning teachers given support to observe their mentors and other colleagues and to be observed by their mentor or other new or veteran colleagues?			
Principal Services			
Do principals model a range of ways of supporting new teachers for their faculty?			
Do principals use a wide range of approaches to enlist all staff in the support of new teachers?			
Do principals use supervision and evaluation as a growth-oriented experience for new teachers?			
School Board and Community			
Do the school committee and parents know that there is a comprehensive induction program in the schools focused on supporting new and veteran teachers for professional growth?			
Is the community invited to support district efforts to support beginning teachers?			
On-going Assessment			
Does the district-wide steering committee engage in on-going assessment of the induction program?			
Does the district-wide steering committee gather summative information on the impact of the induction program and is this information shared with staff and the larger community?			

APPENDIX E

Sample Surveys for Beginning Teachers and Mentors

Informal Survey for Beginning Teachers

*For distribution at beginning teacher networking meetings,
faculty meetings, or other gatherings of staff*

1. What are the three most useful aspects of the program of support for beginning teachers that the district offers?

   _____

   _____

   _____

   _____

   _____

   _____

2. What are the least useful aspects of the program of support for new teachers?

   _____

   _____

   _____

   _____

   _____

   _____

3. What recommendations do you have for our comprehensive induction program?

   _____

   _____

   _____

   _____

   _____

   _____

Informal Survey for Mentors

For distribution at mentor networking meetings,
faculty meetings, or other gatherings of staff

1. What aspects of our mentoring program are the most useful to you
   – and to your beginning teacher?

   _____

   _____

   _____

   _____

   _____

2. From your point of view as a mentor, what are the least useful aspects of the program
   of support for new teachers?

   _____

   _____

   _____

   _____

   _____

3. What recommendations do you have for our comprehensive induction program?

   _____

   _____

   _____

   _____

   _____

APPENDIX F

The Knowledge Base on Teaching

Six Knowledge Bases of Professional Teaching

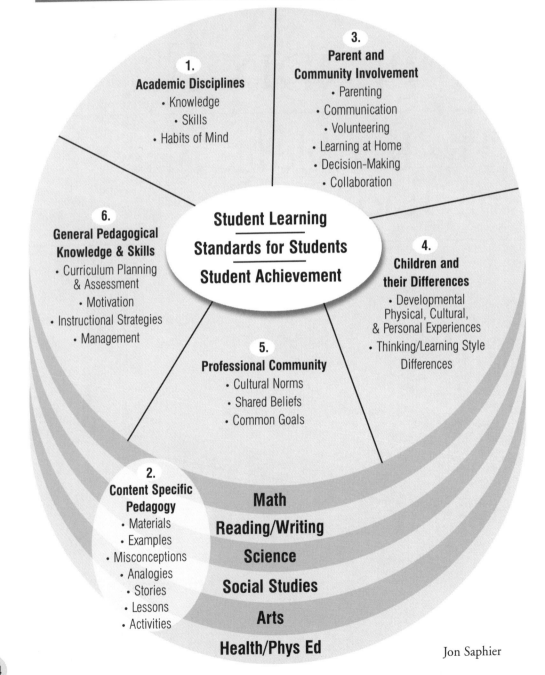

1.
Academic Disciplines
- Knowledge
- Skills
- Habits of Mind

3.
Parent and Community Involvement
- Parenting
- Communication
- Volunteering
- Learning at Home
- Decision-Making
- Collaboration

6.
General Pedagogical Knowledge & Skills
- Curriculum Planning & Assessment
- Motivation
- Instructional Strategies
- Management

Student Learning
Standards for Students
Student Achievement

4.
Children and their Differences
- Developmental Physical, Cultural, & Personal Experiences
- Thinking/Learning Style Differences

5.
Professional Community
- Cultural Norms
- Shared Beliefs
- Common Goals

2.
Content Specific Pedagogy
- Materials
- Examples
- Misconceptions
- Analogies
- Stories
- Lessons
- Activities

Math
Reading/Writing
Science
Social Studies
Arts
Health/Phys Ed

Jon Saphier

Every true profession has a shared knowledge base that grounds its practice. A knowledge base is a baseline set of ideas and concepts essential to high level practice. Every licensed professional is expected to have a working knowledge of these ideas and concepts. In a true profession, a common language and concept system evolves; words are developed to hold the complex meanings of important ideas. This common language facilitates communication; it empowers professional talk between practitioners as they consult and problem-solve with one another.

Obstructing the development of professionalism in teaching is the widespread belief that we do not *have* a knowledge base on teaching at all; that good teaching is an innate endowment. Worse is the parallel belief that teaching is relatively simple work where better teaching comes only from teachers studying content in greater depth - and good pedagogy requires only the acquisition of some simple management and organization strategies. The truth is that teaching is intellectually complex, difficult, and demanding work grounded in a *huge and sophisticated knowledge base* that, if properly conceived, provides endless ground for study and personal growth. Without the proper constructs for what comprises this knowledge base – much less acknowledgement of its existence – true collegiality and experimentation are undercut.

To summarize, we are making the case that acknowledging (or perhaps claiming as our birthright) the professional knowledge base on teaching, which we will frame below, leads to the parallel development of a language and concept system; this language system becomes a cornerstone of teacher learning.

A "knowledge base" has some important characteristics:

- First, it is *organized*. It has certain categories and classifications for the areas acknowledged to be important.

- Second, it is *reliable*. We can count on the information in it because its credibility has been established over time and supported not just by conventional wisdom and the wisdom of practice, but by research.

- Third, it is *adaptable*. It is capable of assimilating new discoveries into its categories or changing the categories if this is warranted by new information.

A knowledge base forms the accumulated foundation of practice and gives professionals a claim to public trust. Being decent and literate are not sufficient qualifications for becoming a member of a knowledge-based profession. The requisite knowledge and skill for teaching cannot be learned casually OTJ – on the job.

The Nature of Professional Knowledge

Policy makers currently operate from a wrong and oversimplified model of what is the knowledge base on teaching. This wrong model has enormous consequences for the structure of schools, for teacher learning, and for induction programs…consequences that inevitably curb reflection and invention and result in widespread mediocrity. The image of teaching in this model starts a chain of actions that lead to treating teachers as low level functionaries whose job it is to "implement" curriculum and decisions that are handed down from above, not to think. This model is the "effectiveness" paradigm that assumes that there is a list of "effective" behaviors that can be identified, learned, and practiced to proficiency. In any true profession, however, the nature of professional knowledge is quite different. It is built around three key concepts:

> 1) areas of performance
>
> 2) repertoire
>
> 3) matching

1) Areas of Performance

There are certain zones of work or areas in which professionals are asked to operate:

- In law...
  One must have competence at writing briefs; taking depositions; filing motions; preparing courtroom strategies.

- In architecture...
  One is called upon to engage in drafting; choosing specifications for beams and trusses; picking an architectural style; interviewing clients to find out what they really want; and making presentations to variance boards for exemptions from local regulations.

2) Repertoire

For each of these areas of performance there is *no one best way of handing things.*

- In law...
  - no single best style for writing a brief
  - no single best courtroom strategy

- In architecture...
  - no one best specification for a main beam
  - no one best way to be persuasive with the zoning board

There exist a *repertoire* of ways to accomplish any task, and no one is inherently better than any other. Queen Ann Victorian homes may be a better match to the tastes of the clients and to the neighborhood than Frank Lloyd Wright modern. Being scientific and precise in pointing out environmental benefits for a project may not be as persuasive with a given zoning board as showing personal concern for the elderly and the needs of the community. Good architects match what they select for a project from a repertoire of options in order to meet the needs of the situation or the client.

3) Matching

In each case, professionals draw from their repertoire the responses that best suit or match the situation. The courtroom strategy is matched to the nature of the case and what is known about the personality of the judge. The design of the house is matched to the contour of the land and to the needs and desires of the owner. The architect is able to bring different house designs and different approaches to each individual case.

These three concepts are defining attributes of professional knowledge in *any* field. Professionals are decision makers; they make decisions from an acquired and ever expanding repertoire. The responses they choose are the ones that are most appropriate to a given situation.

Similarly, in teaching there are many areas of performance. They occur in at least six domains, as profiled in the following pages. Each domain directly bears on student learning.

Domain 1
Academic Disciplines

Deep Knowledge, Skills, Habits of Mind

Teachers of chemistry must continue to expand and deepen their own knowledge of their subject. This not only enables them to bring the latest and best knowledge to their students, but also keeps teachers personally revitalized and enables them to model meaningfully for their students what it means to be a learner. The same can be said for teachers in any discipline.

In the elementary grades, there is likewise a need for teachers to understand at a deep level certain concepts that are embedded in their curricula. For example, the true nature of a "variable" is too little understood by a large portion of elementary teachers. These teachers consider themselves "not scientists," yet are responsible for teaching science to their students.

Liping Ma's groundbreaking book, *Knowing and Teaching Elementary Mathematics* (1999), describes in detail the difference in teaching practice and resulting student understanding that occurs when teachers have what she calls "Profound Understanding of Fundamental Mathematics:"

> *"Based on my research, I define understanding a topic with depth as connecting it with more conceptually powerful ideas of the subject. The closer an idea is to the structure of the discipline, the more powerful it will be. Consequently, the more topics it will be able to support... Depth and*

*breadth…depend on thoroughness — the capacity to
'pass through' all parts of the field — to weave them together.
Indeed, it is this thoroughness which 'glues' knowledge
of mathematics into a coherent whole."*

Deep content knowledge, particularly for elementary teachers, enables them to represent concepts in multiple ways and to tie the concepts together in true teaching for understanding. This deep understanding, perhaps more than any factor, accounts for the differences in mathematics and science instruction noted by Stigler and Heibert (1999) in the TIMMS studies and in their book, *The Teaching Gap*.

In addition to the concepts and skills of the discipline, the thinking skills and habits of mind associated with proficiency in the discipline are essential foundations for good teaching. The recent series by Costa and Kallick on *Habits of Mind* (2000) thoroughly profiles these skills and their implications for teaching.

Studying the content they teach is a necessary and on-going part of the continuing education of all teachers. It must be accommodated in the design of development programs for teachers from initial certification through advanced professional career status.

Domain 2
Content Specific Pedagogy

Materials, Examples, Misconceptions, Analogies, Stories, Activities

For second graders, there is a particular way to use orange and white Cuisenaire rods to illustrate place value; furthermore, there are a set of progressive games for them to play with those materials that are very effective in helping youngsters acquire real understanding of place values and fluency with the notation.

At fifth grade, there is a certain set of practices and procedures that are very effective in helping youngsters learn to develop skills for doing peer editing conferences with each other.

For middle school students, there is a very useful set of materials put out by "The Regional Math Network" under a National Science Foundation grant in 1987 that has realistic word problems that connect with adolescents' interests. Fifteen years later, it is still powerful, though rarely circulated.

The knowledge described above relates to a specific kind of knowledge teachers accumulate over their careers – knowledge of particular materials and particular instructional strategies and procedures for teaching particular content to students of particular ages. Learning these specific methods and materials and how to use them must be a part of the on-going education of professional teachers, whether beginners or veterans. And, as with all professional knowledge, no one example or explanatory device is the right or best one. There is a large repertoire for each concept and skill. Expertise consists of matching one's choices from content specific pedagogy to students and situations.

Part and parcel of this area of knowledge is the fund of good examples and analogies that can be used for particular concepts (e.g. the mailman delivering a bill as an analogy for negative numbers). Teachers also need knowledge of common misconceptions students are liable to bring to instruction (e.g. all rivers flow north to south) so they can be explicitly surfaced, contradicted, and new and accurate conceptions developed.

This kind of knowledge must be part of the professional preparation of teachers. Opportunities to learn this knowledge must be built systematically into both beginning and continuing teacher education.

Lessons, units, and assessments may also be included in this domain. Excellent collections of materials for teaching and assessing specific concepts and skills are available on the Net these days. The skill of being able to design such units and assessments, however, is generic. All teachers should develop this skill in designing to a high level, as we will discuss in Domain 6, Generic Pedagogical Knowledge and Skills.

Domain 3
Parent and Community Involvement

*Parenting, Communication, Volunteering,
Learning at Home, Decision-Making, Collaboration*

Joyce Epstein (1995) and others have profiled the knowledge base on parent and community involvement and its impact on student learning. James Comer (1988) has pointed out the importance of making school a welcoming place for parents as well as students and for the role of parent ownership in governance and change in the school. But this is not an area just for leaders. Teachers particularly need to know about parent involvement and operate from it in their daily practice.

The most important form of parent involvement is involvement in the education of their own children. It makes a huge difference when parents communicate to their own children that they believe education is important and that they (the children) can do well if they work hard and use good strategies. Teachers can learn a great deal about the skills and strategies of effective communication with parents and about ways to augment parents' ability to reinforce the message about working hard to achieve success at school. Teacher education in the 21st century, especially in urban areas, needs to include knowledge and skill at reaching parents and finding ways to involve them constructively in the life of the school and in the education of their own youngsters.

Domain 4
Children and Their Differences

*Developmental Physical, Cultural and Personal Experiences,
Thinking/Learning Style Differences*

Domain 4 is the study of differences – differences in learners. Understanding and adjusting for differences in learners calls for the highest level of artistry from teachers as they draw on the repertoire they have developed in all other strands to optimize learning environments for students. It is in this domain that the all important issues of child development are addressed, including cognitive and emotional development. This knowledge is essential to good "matching" as teachers make selections from their own teaching repertoire.

There are also other kinds of differences that are very important for teachers to understand.

- Differences in learning style, including perceptual preferences and the ways individuals process information. Adjusting instruction for these differences and teaching students to use knowledge of their own learning styles to their advantage can significantly enhance learning rate and retention. Learning these strategies should be part of teacher training.

- Differences in cultural style among youngsters of different ethnic and regional heritages. The cultural backgrounds of children's homes can have significant impact on the attitudes and approaches youngsters bring to school. Teachers should bring an understanding of these differences to instruction.

- Differences of race, color, and language that influence students' self-concept as learners, their approach to school, and their approaches to others who are different from themselves. As we become a nation where the minorities are the majority, it is crucial that teachers help students to cultivate appreciation of their differences rather than rejection or suspicion of those differences from oneself. Good teacher education curricula should educate teachers specifically about these differences and how to help students deal with them positively.

Domain 5
Professional Community

Cultural Norms, Shared Beliefs, Common Goals

This domain of the knowledge base focuses on the individual's participation, influence, and initiative in the "system" of the school. We know that the school as a whole is a system that has a strong impact on the learning of the child; teachers are members of that larger system. Study of this knowledge base enables teachers to understand the school district as a community and to play active and positive roles in strengthening the school as a whole. One area of this knowledge base is awareness of the norms of a school culture that comprise a healthy growth-oriented workplace for adults – and knowledge of how to build and strengthen these norms.

A second area of this knowledge base is how to participate actively with one's team to come up with – for example – common proficiency targets for students with exemplars, aligned curriculum, and assessments. A third area is the beliefs that are known to ground what Newmann and Wehlage (1999) call "academic press" for all students: the willingness to push and stretch students with persistence, tenacity, and caring support. A map of this knowledge base can be found on Figures 5 and 6.

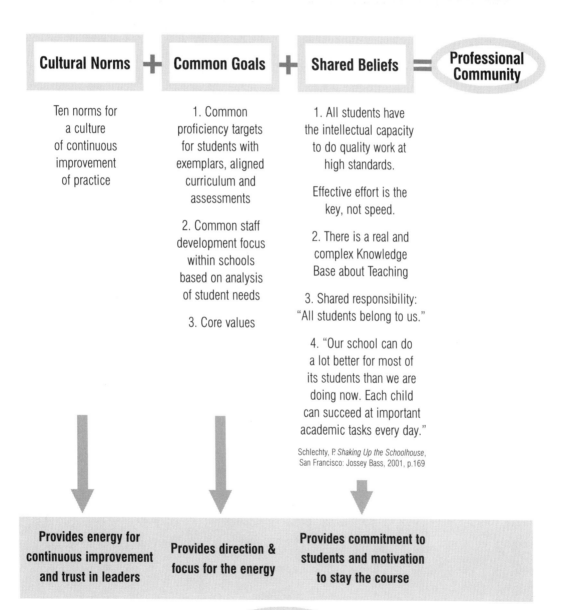

Defining Professional Community for Increasing Student Achievement

Cultural Norms + **Common Goals** + **Shared Beliefs** = **Professional Community**

Cultural Norms

Ten norms for a culture of continuous improvement of practice

Common Goals

1. Common proficiency targets for students with exemplars, aligned curriculum and assessments

2. Common staff development focus within schools based on analysis of student needs

3. Core values

Shared Beliefs

1. All students have the intellectual capacity to do quality work at high standards.

Effective effort is the key, not speed.

2. There is a real and complex Knowledge Base about Teaching

3. Shared responsibility: "All students belong to us."

4. "Our school can do a lot better for most of its students than we are doing now. Each child can succeed at important academic tasks every day."

Schlechty, P. *Shaking Up the Schoolhouse*, San Francisco: Jossey Bass, 2001, p.169

Provides energy for continuous improvement and trust in leaders

Provides direction & focus for the energy

Provides commitment to students and motivation to stay the course

Figure 5.

Ten Cultural Norms of Professional Community

The D.N.A... Requisite norms that allow all the others to develop	What "collaboration" really means: norms which result directly in improved instruction and better student achievement	Important background norms that generate affiliation and commitment
1 **Honest, Open Communication**	**3** **Non-Defensive Self-Examination of Teaching Practice**	**7** **Protecting What's Important**
	4 **Systematic Examination of Data**	**8** **Appreciation & Recognition**
2 **Involvement in Decision-Making**	**5** **Reaching Out to the Knowledge Base**	**9** **Celebration, Caring, Humor, Traditions, Rituals, Ceremonies**
	6 **Experimentation, Analysis & Self-Critique in Groups** Groups of teachers who share students and/or content demonstrate these behaviors in their meetings.	**10** **High Expectations & Accountability for Adults**

Figure 6.

Domain 6
Generic Pedagogical Knowledge & Skills

Management, Motivation, Instructional Strategies,
Curriculum Planning & Assessment

It is a paradox that the knowledge base on pedagogy is enormous, complex, rich, subtle, and vital to successful teaching – and yet it is barely present in teacher education. In fact, its very existence is frequently denied.

The knowledge base on generic pedagogy is clear, explicit, and can be understood, like any professional knowledge base, in terms of categories or areas of performance, each of which is important in its own right for successful teaching and learning. Domain 6, Generic Pedagogical Knowledge, can be grouped into four categories, **Motivation, Management, Instructional Strategies**, and **Curriculum Planning**, which are described below. It is essential that all professional teachers show high levels of competence in these areas if we are to educate all our children to 21st century standards. Each area is important and contains repertoires of very specific behaviors and patterns of thought that can be learned, practiced, and applied. When added together, they comprise the tools of a highly complex knowledge base that gets applied through analysis, problem-solving, and the capacity to draw from one's repertoire a response that is appropriate to the situation. They are grouped in four categories and eighteen sub-categories that have been validated empirically (Saphier, 1980) and though by no means sacred, are a convenient set for holding the range and complexity of interactive teaching (Saphier, 1999).

These four areas of knowledge comprise the larger category of Generic Pedagogical Knowledge and are necessary but not sufficient conditions for successful teaching.

1. Knowledge of Motivation is what teachers use to influence students' desire to learn, their belief that it would be worthwhile to do so, and that they have the capacity to succeed with high level material if they try. With knowledge of motivation, teachers develop understandings and skills on how to make students feel significant and capable. Teachers are also able to demonstrate to students that the content is worth learning and that the teacher cares about their personal welfare and success.

2. Management Knowledge is about enabling, attaining, and sustaining engagement with academic tasks and about anticipating and removing obstacles to this engagement.

3. Knowledge of Instructional Strategies means mastering powerful tools for helping students construct knowledge, anchor their learning, and connect learning to their lives.

4. Knowledge of Curriculum Planning means developing the capacity in teachers to be rigorous and complex curriculum thinkers – architects of experiences that have continuity, appropriate sequencing, and integration with other disciplines so that students see these learning experiences as relevant to life and connected to other kinds of knowledge.

BIBLIOGRAPHY

Bartell, C., & Ownby, L. (1994). *Report on the Implementation of the Beginning Teacher Support and Assessment Program,* 1992-1994. Sacramento, CA: California Commission on New Teacher Credentialing and California Department of Education.

Benner, P. (2000). *From Novice to Expert: Excellence and Power in Clinical Nursing.* New Jersey: Prentice Hall.

Bereiter, C. and Scardamalia, M. (1993). *Surpassing Ourselves – An Inquiry into the Nature and Implications of Expertise.* Chicago: Open Court.

Berliner, D. (1987). "Ways of Thinking about Students and Classrooms by More and Less Experienced Teachers," in J. Calderhead (ed.), *Exploring Teachers' Thinking.* London: Cassell.

Comer, J. (1988). "Educating Poor Minority Children." *Scientific American.* 259: 42-48.

Costa, A. L. and Garmston, R. J. (1994). *Cognitive Coaching: A Foundation for Renaissance Schools.* Norwood, MA: Christopher Gordon.

Costa, A. L. and Kallick, B. (2000). *Discovering and Exploring Habits of Mind.* Alexandria, VA: ASCD.

Costa, A. L. and Kallick, B. (2000). *Activating and Enjoying Habits of Mind* (Habits of Mind, Book 2). Alexandria, VA: ASCD.

Costa, A. L. and Kallick, B. (2000). *Assessing and Reporting on Habits of Mind* (Habits of Mind, Book 3). Alexandria, VA: ASCD.

Costa, A. L. and Kallick, B. (2000). *Integrating and Sustaining Habits of Mind* (Habits of Mind, Book 4). Alexandria, VA: ASCD.

Darling-Hammond, L. (1996). *What Matters Most: Teaching for America's Future.* New York: National Commission on Teaching and America's Future.

Darling-Hammond, L. (1997). *Doing What Matters Most: Investing in Quality Teaching.* New York: National Commission on Teaching and America's Future.

Darling-Hammond, L. (2000). *Solving the Dilemmas of Teacher Supply and Quality.* New York: National Commission on Teaching and America's Future.

Darling-Hammond, L. (2001). "The Challenge of Staffing Our Schools," *Educational Leadership,* ASCD.

Dreyfus, H. L. and Dreyfus, S. E. (1986). *Mind over Machine.* New York: Free Press.

Educational Leadership. (May, 1999). This issue is devoted to "Supporting New Teachers." Volume 56, Number 8.

Educational Leadership. (May, 2001). This issue is devoted to "Who is Teaching our Children?" Volume 58, Number 8.

Edwards, J. (1994). "Thinking, Education and Human Potential." In J. Edwards, ed., *Thinking: International Interdisciplinary Perspectives.* Melbourne: Hawker Brownlow Education.

Epstein, J. L. (1995). "School/Family/Community Partnerships," *Phi Delta Kappan.* May, 1995.

Feiman-Nemser, S. & Parker, M. (1993). "Mentoring in Context: A Comparison of Two U.S. Programs for Beginning Teachers." *International Journal of Educational Research,* 19(8), 699-718.

Fideler, E. & Haselkorn, D. (2000). *Learning the Ropes: Urban teacher induction programs and practices in the United States.* Belmont, MA: Recruiting New Teachers, Inc.

Glickman, C. (2000). *SuperVision and Instructional Leadership: A Developmental Approach.* Boston: Allyn and Bacon.

Gold, Y. (1996). "Beginning Teacher Support: Attrition, Mentoring and Induction." In J. Sikula, T.J. Buttery, and E. Guyton (eds.), *Handbook of Research on Teacher Education.* New York: Macmillan.

Gregorian, Vartan. (2001). Op Ed Article, *New York Times,* July 9, 2001.

Gross, S. (1999). *Elementary Science in Montgomery County Maryland: A Comprehensive Transformation of a System Wide Screener Program.* ESI 91-53827. Maryland: Montgomery County Public Schools.

Harrison, A.F. and Bramson, R. M. (1982). *The Art of Thinking.* New York: Berkeley Books.

Hersey, P., Blanchard, K. H., and Johnson, D. E. (2000). *Management of Organizational Behavior: Leading Human Resources.* New Jersey: Prentice Hall.

Huling-Austin. L. (1990). "Teacher Induction Programs and Internships." In R. W. Houston (ed.), *Handbook of Research on Teacher Education.* New York: Macmillan.

Little, J. W. (1982). "Norms of Collegiality and Experimentation: Workplace Conditions of School Success." *Education Research Journal.* 19(3) 325-340.

Little, J. W. (1993). "Teachers' Professional Development in a Climate of Educational Reform." *Educational Evaluation and Policy Analysis,* 15(2), 129-151.

Ma, L. (1999). *Knowing and Teaching Elementary Mathematics: Teachers' Understanding of Fundamental Mathematics in China and the United States.* New Jersey: Lawrence Erlbaum Associates.

National Association of State Boards of Education. (1998). *The Numbers Game: Ensuring Quantity and Quality in the Teaching Work Force.* Alexandria, VA: Author.

Newmann, F. and Wehlage, F. (1999). *Successful School Restructuring.* Wisconsin: University of Wisconsin Press.

Odell, S. J. (1986). "Induction Support of New Teachers: A Fundamental Approach." *Journal of Teacher Education.* 37(1): 26-29.

Odell, S. J. and Ferraro, D. P. (1992). "Teacher Mentoring and Teacher Retention." *Journal of Teacher Education.* 43(3): 201-204.

Platt, A., et al. (1999). *The Skillful Leader: Confronting Mediocre Teaching*. Acton, MA: Author.

Rosenholtz, S. J. (1989). *Teachers' Workplace: The Social Organization of Schools*. New York: Longman.

Sanders, W.L. and Reeves, J.C. (1998). "Cumulative and Residual Effects of Teachers on Future Student Academic Achievement." In *Thinking K-16: Good Teaching Matters. How Well Qualified Teachers Can Close the Gap*. Education Trust.

Saphier, J. (1980). *The Parameters of Teaching: An Empirical Study Using Observations and Interviews to Validate a Theory of Teaching by Linking Levels of Analysis, Levels of Knowing, and Levels of Performance*. Doctoral Dissertation: Boston University.

Saphier, J. (1993). *How to Make Supervision and Evaluation Really Work*. Carlisle, MA: Research for Better Teaching.

Saphier, J. and Gower, R. (1997) *The Skillful Teacher*. Carlisle, MA: Research for Better Teaching.

Scherer, M. (Ed.). (1999). *A Better Beginning*. Alexandria, VA: ASCD.

Shulman, L. (1986). "Those Who Understand: Knowledge Growth in Teaching." *Educational Researcher,* 15(2):4-14.

Stigler, J. W. and Hiebert, J. (1988). *The Learning Gap*. New York: Summit Books.

Sweeney, B. A. (1998). "A survey of the 50 state-mandated novice teacher programs: Implications for state and local mentoring programs and practices." On-line: www.teachermentors.com

"Who Should Teach?" (January 12, 2000). *Educational Leadership,* ASCD.

Wiggins, G. and McTighe, J. (1998). *Understanding by Design*. Alexandria, VA: ASCD.

Wong, H. K. (August 8, 2001). "Mentoring Can't Do It All: New teachers learn best from systematic induction programs." *Education Week*. On-line: www.newteacher.com

Web Sites for New Educators

A homepage for new English/Language Arts teachers
www.ncte.org

Click on TEACH2000

This site offers a variety of resources and a free subscription to new language arts teachers.

A homepage for new math teachers
www.clarityconnect/webpages/terri/terri.html

This site is filled with ideas for new (and not so new) math teachers and includes math problems for students, Internet guidelines, resources, and professional suggestions.

Beginning Teacher's Tool Box
www.inspiringteachers.com

Beginning teachers can leave a message for a cyber-mentor or subscribe to Pencil Points, a newsletter written for and by teachers.

FIRSTYEARS
www.subscribe-request@netpals/soft.com

A free e-mail subscription dedicated to beginning teachers.

Iloveteaching.com
www.iloveteaching.com

This site is authored by a "new" teacher (six years of experience) who is interested in encouraging other new teachers.

Recruiting New Teachers
www.rnt.org

This site offers guidance and resources to prospective teachers. It also includes the executive summary of "Learning the Ropes," a report produced by Recruiting New Teachers.

Teachers Helping Teachers
www.pacificnet.net/~mandel

This site offers basic tips for beginning teachers and is a curriculum resource for lesson plans and links to education sites, organized by subject and topic.

The New Teacher Page
www.new-teacher.com

This site contains information, advice, and ideas specific to new and aspiring educators. Has a variety of links to educators' sites.

The Ultimate Teacher's Resource
www.teachers.net

This site offers lesson plans, a newsletter, and a bookshelf of resources.

What to expect in your first year of teaching
www.ed.gov/pubs/FirstYear

This site offers suggestions and support through vignettes of new teachers in real situations.

World Wide Web Resources for New Teachers
www.public.asu.edu/~dsalce/sed403/sed403.htm

This site links to general education sites, lesson plans, educational journals, and AskEric.

INDEX

ABOUT TEACHERS[21] AND THE AUTHORS

About TEACHERS²¹

This booklet sets forth a vision and model for the comprehensive induction of beginning teachers that is implemented by *Teachers*²¹ in its consulting work with teachers and administrators in urban, suburban, and rural school districts.

*Teachers*²¹ is a non-profit national center for the professionalizing of teaching that is taking leadership in strengthening the role of teachers in the educational process. Founded by Jon Saphier, *Teachers*²¹ is working to align and strengthen the systems – teacher recruitment, preparation, induction, and on-going professional development – at the national, state, and district levels that have the capacity for improving teaching and student learning.

*Teachers*²¹ is committed to two underlying propositions:

- Teaching is one of the most complex human endeavors.
- A key factor in effective student learning is what the teacher knows, believes, and is able to do.

Drawing on a commitment to the knowledge base on teaching that it shares with its partner organization, Research for Better Teaching (RBT), *Teachers*²¹ is dedicated to strengthening the practice of teaching by new and experienced teachers and the leadership of systemic school improvement by administrators.

In collaboration with Simmons College, *Teachers*²¹ has established the Beginning Teacher Center for expanding the skills and confidence of beginning teachers in order to advance learning in their classrooms; increase the retention of new teachers; and foster communication among college education faculty and school practitioners.

*Teachers*²¹ provides direct services that strengthen teachers' and administrators' understanding of the professional skills and knowledge that are essential to teaching and administration and expand districts' capacity to provide coherent and on-going staff development. *Teachers*²¹ is developing an electronic library that reflects the best professional knowledge on teaching and provides educators with proven strategies for improving student learning.

Jon Saphier

Jon Saphier is the Founder and Chairman of the Board of *Teachers*[21], a non-profit organization dedicated to strengthening teaching as a profession. Jon is also the Founder of Research for Better Teaching, a former classroom teacher, and a nationally respected staff developer and consultant. Dr. Saphier is the author of six books, including *The Skillful Teacher*, and numerous articles on staff development, supervision and evaluation, and school culture.

Susan Freedman

Susan Freedman is the President of *Teachers*[21] and co-founder of the Beginning Teacher Center of *Teachers*[21] and Simmons College. She is a former member of the National Commission on Families, Communities, Schools, and Children's Learning and a former public school teacher. Susan is a former educational consultant working with districts across the country and the author and co-author of numerous publications on school restructuring and school improvement.

Barbara Aschheim

Barbara Aschheim is the Vice-President of *Teachers*[21], a former public school teacher and higher education administrator. She is a staff developer who has worked with teachers and administrators in over 120 school districts on developing and implementing comprehensive induction programs for new teachers. Barbara is the co-author of numerous publications and articles on school-community partnerships and school improvement.